GO AHEAD IN THE RAIN

AMERICAN MUSIC SERIES

David Menconi, Jessica Hopper, Oliver Wang, Editors

Go Ahead in the Rain

NOTES TO A TRIBE CALLED QUEST

HANIF ABDURRAQIB

UNIVERSITY OF TEXAS PRESS ☙ AUSTIN

The author would like to thank Cheryl Boyce-Taylor for generously granting
permission to excerpt from "A Woman Speaks" and reprint in full "Devouring
the Light, 1968."

"Do Not Forget Old Friends" by Leonard Cohen, collected in *Selected Poems:
1956–1968*. Copyright © 1974 Leonard Cohen, used by permission of The Wylie
Agency LLC.

Requests for permission to reproduce material from this work should be sent to:
    Permissions
    University of Texas Press
    P.O. Box 7819
    Austin, TX 78713-7819
    utpress.utexas.edu/rp-form

♾ The paper used in this book meets the minimum requirements of ANSI/NISO
Z39.48-1992 (R1997) (Permanence of Paper).

Library of Congress Cataloging-in-Publication Data

Names: Abdurraqib, Hanif, author.
Title: Go ahead in the rain : notes to A Tribe Called Quest / Hanif Abdurraqib.
Description: Austin : University of Texas Press, 2019.
Identifiers: LCCN 2018031799
    ISBN 978-1-4773-1648-1 (pbk. : alk. paper)
    ISBN 978-1-4773-1843-0 (library e-book)
    ISBN 978-1-4773-1844-7 (non-library e-book)
Subjects: LCSH: Tribe Called Quest (Musical group) | Rap
musicians—United States—Biography.
Classification: LCC ML421.T762 W55 2019 | DDC 782.421649092/2—dc23
LC record available at https://lccn.loc.gov/2018031799

doi:10.7560/316481

Contents

GO AHEAD IN THE RAIN

CHAPTER ONE

The Paths of Rhythm

In the beginning, from somewhere south of anywhere I come from, lips pressed the edge of a horn, and a horn was blown. In the beginning before the beginning, there were drums, and hymns, and a people carried here from another here, and a language stripped and a new one learned, with the songs to go with it. When slaves were carried to America, stolen from places like West Africa and the greater Congo River, with them came a musical tradition. The tradition, generally rooted in one-line melodies and call-and-response, existed to allow the rhythms within the music to reflect African speech patterns—in part so that everyone who had a voice could join in on the music making, which made music a community act instead of an exclusive one.

Once in America, where the slaves were sent to work in

America's South, this ethos was blended with the harmonic style of the Baptist church. Black slaves learned hymns, blended them with their own musical stylings that had been passed down through generations, and thus, the spiritual was born. In the early nineteenth century, free black musicians began picking up and playing European stringed instruments, particularly violin. It started as a joke—to mimic European dance music during black cakewalk dances. But even the mimicry sounded sweet, and so the children of slaves made what sweet sounds they could and stole a small and precious thing after having a large and precious history stolen from them.

But before this, when slaves were first brought to North America in the early 1600s, slaves from the West African coast would use drums to communicate with each other, sending rhythmic messages that could not be decoded by Europeans. In this way, slaves, whose family members were often held captive in different spaces, could still enter into distant but meaningful conversations with one another. In 1740, the slave codes were enacted, first in South Carolina. Among other things, drums were outlawed for all slaves. Slave Code of South Carolina, Article 36 reads: "And . . . it is absolutely necessary to the safety of this Province, that all due care be taken to restrain . . . Negroes and other slaves . . . [from the] using or keeping of drums, horns, or other loud instruments, which may call together or give sign or notice to one another of their wicked designs and purposes."

The slave codes spread across plantations, first to the Carolinas, and then Georgia, and then the rest of the United States.

Wherever there were slaves or their descendants, drums were torn from the spaces they occupied.

The thing about percussion, which remains true today as children still pound fists on lunch tables to stretch a simple beat into something greater, is that all it takes is a surface and rhythm—a closed fist or an open palm and something merciful enough to be trampled upon. Without drums, slaves would make beats on washboards, available furniture, even their own bodies, finding the hollow and forgiving spots with the most echo. They would stomp and holler. The voice, too, is its own type of percussion—particularly when it is used to rattle the sky on a hot day, when there is endless work resting at your feet. The work is also an instrument—the way the wood can be chopped is a percussion and the march to the work is a percussion and the weary chants, when laid close enough to one another, can be a percussion.

When they took the drums of slaves, the slaves simply found new drums in everything, and this is how African rhythms were retained and passed down, held close by those who knew what it was to have a culture ripped from them.

Jazz, then, is a music born out of necessity. When slavery was abolished in 1865, many former slaves went into entertainment with all they had: the music knowledge they'd kept as a means of staying alive, blended with what other black musicians had learned along the way. By the end of the nineteenth century, ragtime was born, and from ragtime sprang the blues, and somewhere in the middle appeared Charles "Buddy" Bolden, who played what would become jazz, who mixed ragtime and the blues together and improvised with his band in the early 1900s down south in New Orleans before he got drunk and fell unconscious at the New Orleans Labor Day Parade in 1906 and never recovered.

Buddy Bolden, a cornet player from New Orleans, is as much a myth as anything. He built his band by learning how to mix instruments from local New Orleans bands that played blues and ragtime separately but never together. From 1900 to 1906, he was the king of a new sound, before alcohol rendered him largely incapable of keeping up with the demand to make new music. No sound recording of Buddy Bolden exists. In 1907, he was overtaken by what is now known as schizophrenia. Buddy Bolden heard voices and was locked away in a New Orleans asylum for twenty-four years until he died, buried in an unmarked grave in a pauper's graveyard.

It can be said that the entire story of jazz is actually a story about what can urgently be passed down to someone else before a person expires. Jazz was created by a people obsessed with their survival in a time that did not want them to survive, and so it is a genre of myths—of fantasy and dreaming, of drumming on whatever you must and making noise in any way you can, before the ability to make noise is taken from you, or until the noise is an echo in your own head that won't rest.

In the beginning, I played the trumpet as a boy because in a picture I saw from a time I can't remember, Miles Davis was slouched in a black leather chair in a white suit, the jacket unbuttoned and gold chains resting across his black skin. In his left hand, he held a bloodred horn, his name engraved on the side of it in gold. I saw Miles Davis and I decided that he was cool. I first loved what I understood as jazz because the coolness inside it was an unspoken act. I was a shy and nervous kid, wracked with anxiety before I understood what anxiety was. I was desperate for a way to wear silence in a way that looked and felt cool to anyone in my presence.

My father played instruments, several of them well, but not well enough to strike out and start a band. He played drums, clarinet, keyboard, and, later, an alto saxophone. Some evenings, if the day had been particularly long, he would retreat to the basement and put on old jazz records: John Coltrane, Charles Mingus, Eric Dolphy, Miles Davis. I imagine it was the lack of spoken language in the music that drew him to it—the understanding that not all silence is silence. I would, at times, sit at the top of the steps and listen, building my own language from the sounds.

And so, in the beginning, I played the trumpet as a boy to bridge a gap between my father and me. This gap wasn't particularly tense or rooted in any conflict, but that somehow made it more difficult to navigate. When there is nothing to point to as an excuse for distance, the distance looms larger, more difficult to push.

At the music store, I picked out a used silver trumpet, much to my father's delight. I was heading into the sixth grade, eager to find new ways to fit in and hoping a musical skill would be my entry point. I started taking lessons with Dr. Robert Parish, a music teacher who taught on the east side of Columbus, Ohio. He had already trained both my father and my older brother, and he was thrilled to take me on.

It was never the reading of the music that turned me off—I loved the intricacies of the notes from a young age.

As someone who found joy in reading, to read and unravel notes of music was a pleasure for me. To translate them into actual sound, however, was a discouraging practice. Like many young people who get an idea, I quickly became disinterested once I realized that practicing the trumpet cut into the time I could have spent outside with my friends. My father had me set aside an hour a day—a reasonable request, but one that I constantly found loopholes in. I would wait until right before my father made it home before I started playing, blowing out the last few notes of "Autumn Leaves" as he walked in the door, in hopes that it would convince him that I'd put in my time. This worked until, of course, Dr. Parish realized I wasn't getting any better over time. It became obvious that I wasn't practicing at home.

Yet, I joined my middle school jazz band, hoping that I could sneak an easy grade onto my report card by hiding behind the more skilled players assembled there. The teacher was a white man. I carried my beaten-up trumpet case to school with me every day, the smell of valve oil permeating through the school bus on the days I'd clean the trumpet in the morning. Cleaning it was my favorite part—to restore it back to its original self, briefly seeing my face in the silver. It was in these moments that I most felt like Miles Davis, leaned back in his leather chair, holding his shiny horn, knowing he was the master of it.

For the best jazz players, the instrument is an extension of the body. I never allowed myself to understand this part. The trumpet was a beautiful instrument to me, and I did not imagine myself to be beautiful. To hold it was to hold something that still felt foreign. To press my lips to it felt like a reckless and unearned intimacy. Thus, the trumpet was always an unnatural experience for me, even though I tried to make it part of me for longer than I should have. It was less about what I wanted, and more about what I felt I deserved.

In seventh grade jazz band, I struggled to grasp my solos, missing notes and squeaking out weak notes that should have been loud, boastful, and brilliant. The teacher, in year two of having me as a student, suggested that I try another instrument. His reasoning was simple: my lips were simply too big to play the trumpet.

In the moment, this was a blessing for me to hear. Finally, a reason for my failure to make this beautiful instrument bend to my will. I went home and excitedly told my father the news: I could no longer play trumpet because my lips were too big to play it well. My father immediately flew into a subdued but palpable rage. Having been alive for so long, used to workplaces and spaces where navigating racist microaggressions was a part of an everyday routine, he saw to the heart of the issue. The next day, he demanded a meeting with the teacher.

Before dragging me to the school, he shuffled around the house compiling a stack of records: trumpet players Louis Armstrong, Lee Morgan, Wynton Marsalis, Donald Byrd, Freddie Hubbard, and sax player Eric Dolphy, all black. When we arrived, without sitting, he spread all of the records out on the teacher's desk. He'd point to the back covers of the albums, some of them showing portraits of the musicians with no instruments attached to their faces. "Look at these lips," he'd say, hitting the back of an album with his palm. "You think these lips are too big to play trumpet?" And there were Eric Dolphy's full lips, staring back, answering the question on their own. Or Louis Armstrong, whose lips were even fuller than my own, grinning knowingly into the room's silence. The teacher was stunned, surely not expecting a student's father to ask him to answer for a racist slight. But, for me, the damage had already been done. Underneath my relief to imagine myself done with the trumpet was shame. For so long, I had considered myself undeserving of such a beautiful instrument. To hear it made plain—to be told that my body was, indeed, not made for it—was first comforting and then deflating. Yes, of course, I remember thinking. Of course I am not worthy of this glorious machine.

As I look back now, I know that for my father, this was something greater. I imagine that he, too, knew that my trumpet playing was a lost cause. He'd heard me failing at it, and I suspect that he knew I was sneaking the timing of my practices to appease him. My father wanted to defend me against the teacher's slight, I'm sure. But even beyond that, he wanted to defend a history that he knew and understood. He wanted to defend the sounds that got him through his long days and the language that he could walk into easier than most others. This is the thing about history and people who come from a people who have had it taken from them. They know if they don't protect what they can, there will be nothing to pass on to their children. Even when their children can't get through a simple jazz standard.

This was all during the time of the Walkman, or if you had money—which my family didn't—the early days of the

Discman. In my headphones, most days, I played the albums of A Tribe Called Quest, the rap group from Queens, New York. Rap in my household oscillated between taboo and acceptable, depending on the year or the mood my parents were in, or if they'd decided to give up altogether and leave their four children to their own musical devices. Still, no matter what vibe they were on, the early albums of A Tribe Called Quest were acceptable to play in the house. It isn't so much that my parents listened to them actively, but the sound of their songs felt like something acceptable—warm and vital.

The first song of *The Low End Theory*, A Tribe Called Quest's second album, is "Excursions." The spine of the song is a slow galloping bassline, a jazz sample from Art Blakey and the Jazz Messenger's "A Chant for Bu." I played that song the most during my brief flirtation with undertaking jazz music. It seemed an entire world away from anything on the first Tribe album, 1990's *People's Instinctive Travels and the Paths of Rhythm*, which was a vital introduction to the group's ethos but didn't resonate as thoroughly in Columbus, Ohio, in the summer months after it came out. That album had a jazzlike pace and feel to it, but *The Low End Theory* was the one that absorbed itself in the music, committing itself to almost being a jazz album.

"Excursions" is the first rap song I knew that could sound good in almost any situation: in headphones, in the background on any night with a thick and heavy moon hanging above your head, in a car with the windows rolled down on a hot day. The relationship with bass in rap music, to that point, had been more computerized than instrumental.

As an introduction to the shape of rap to come, here was A Tribe Called Quest, on their sophomore album, repurposing a bass guitar that was once played with someone's hands dancing across the strings.

In the beginning, both after and before a new series of beginnings, there was a rap group from Queens composed of Q-Tip, the Abstract, with his nasally and introspective flow—a world builder with a deft touch and endless vision; Phife Dawg, Five-Foot Assassin, with his penchant for wordplay and punch lines; Ali Shaheed Muhammad; and Jarobi White, the brains and the backbone of the group.

What made A Tribe Called Quest special is that if one looks closely enough, it is possible to believe that they were sent here directly by some wild-dreaming ancestors, straight from another era. They felt like old souls, even when they were young. When I put my trumpet into its case for the last time, and tucked it into a closet somewhere, I played *The Low End Theory* for months on end, wondering if I'd ever stop. This was the jazz I had been looking for: an album that blended horns and funk the same way Bolden blended ragtime and blues and was seamless in its execution. *The Low End Theory* sampled Dolphy, Sly Stone, Weather Report, Julian Cannonball Adderley, and Jimi Hendrix, among others. The Tribe was one of the first groups to repurpose a long line of sound that our parents, and perhaps their parents, were in love with. There is a type of mercy in this honoring: a long reach backward toward something magical, in hopes that an unspeakable distance, perhaps between a parent and a child, can slowly become closer.

I loved A Tribe Called Quest because I wore hand-me-down

jeans to school, my clothes were sometimes too big, and I didn't make eye contact when I spoke, so I was decidedly weird. They, too, were walking a thin line of weirdness: just weird enough to stand out from their peers, but not so weird that it seemed to be contrived. The jazz, in some ways, made them cool. They wore baggy sweatshirts in music videos with all of their friends. Early on, particularly for their first two albums, it didn't seem like they were angling for anything other than their own moment: a chance to recall some of the musical archives that they once held close, with very little interest in a relationship to the mainstream. Perhaps, they knew that the closer they carried their unique relationship with that sound to the light, the more chance it had to be taken away.

Tucked into the middle of *The Low End Theory* is the second single, "Jazz (We've Got)." I remember the music video, seeping from the television late on a Saturday night during *Yo! MTV Raps*. Everyone talks about the end of the video, when the music video and song transition to "Buggin' Out" and the enduring image of Phife Dawg and Q-Tip with miniature white cups over their eyes, giving off the odd impression of cartoonish and large bulging discs in the place of their normal-sized eyes. But the first part of the video, the bulk of it, is the most enduring. The group walks around New York City in a haze of black and white, rapping in simplistic fashion about the nuances of jazz music. It is an easy relic of a time past when watched now, and it was easy to dismiss in the moment. When discussing the single on the school bus, the older kids would dismissively wave their hands and say things like "I'm not listening to this shit! This the kinda shit old people like!"

And perhaps that is true. A Tribe Called Quest made rap music for our parents and theirs but left the door open wide enough for anyone to sneak through. Anyone with rhythm or anyone who knew how to find it before the bass high-stepped itself across a dance floor. Q-Tip, in the first verse of "Jazz," sums it up evenly: "I don't really mind if it's over your head / 'Cause the job of resurrectors is to wake up the dead."

So this is the story of A Tribe Called Quest, proficient in many arts but none greater than the art of resurrections—a group that faced the past until the present became too enticing for them to ignore. Of how I found myself beautiful enough for jazz music, but only in their image and nowhere else. Of how, in the Midwest, their songs first did not play out of passing cars but then played everywhere. Of how you can be both uncool and desirable all at once. Here, a story begins even before jazz. Like all black stories in America, it begins first with what a people did to amend their loss in light of what they no longer had at their disposal. With an open palm against a chest, or a closed fist against a washboard, or a voice, echoing into a vast and oppressive sky, or an album teeming with homages—here is the story of how, even without our drums, we still find a way to speak to each other across any distance placed between us.

CHAPTER TWO

Once Upon a Time in Queens

It is much easier to determine when rap music became political and significantly more difficult to pinpoint when it became dangerous. There is a belief, I'm sure, that it is impossible to imagine a world in which those two things were not always on a course toward each other, especially if you believe that everything is political. I don't think the house party is always political, at least not as a universal element—though it might be political for someone who is finding their own small piece of freedom within a party's walls. But the first bits of hip-hop were born out of DJs breaking apart funk and disco beats and relegating every other sound to a graveyard until all that was left was the percussion, cut up into small, danceable portions for the people in the audience to sweat to. And sweat is sometimes political. Say, if it comes off the back of someone who is working in a field that is not their own field in a country that wasn't always their country. Sweat is sometimes political when it falls from the shoulders of an athlete who is playing for a college in a place where they might be one of few black people on campus. But sweat isn't always political—not when it's the small river being formed between two warm bodies in the midst of some block party or basement or anywhere music is coming from hands touched to records.

To DJ is hard work, and it can be argued that DJs were also composers—not in the sense of classical music composers, but a case can be made that early hip-hop DJs not only had to find the right groove in an old record but also had to know when to unleash that groove onto a room to get the bodies vibrating at the correct pitch. It's easy to reduce touching fingers to vinyl to a simple act. But it is, in a way, commanding an orchestra, an orchestra of skin to skin and yes, sweat. But even with this in mind, the art of the turntable is not inherently political.

The lights went out in New York City in July 1977. Lightning struck an electricity transmission line in the heart of the city, causing the line's automatic circuit breaker to kick in. The initial lightning strike wasn't the problem—it was the second one, which struck about twenty minutes after the first, hitting an electrical substation in Yonkers, which took out two more transmission lines. At some point, if anything is pushed far enough, it is impossible to sustain.

To "shed a load"—in the electrical sense—means to do away with voltage. Electric companies lower their overall voltage use in order to spare some power for the entire grid. In other words, it's a disposal of energy. It goes nowhere in particular.

It just vanishes. Con Edison tried to shed the load to save the city from a massive blackout. And it worked at first, with engineers lowering voltage across the board in a series of events that allowed them to reduce the overall load. But a problem occurred in the chain reaction of substations tripping in Upstate New York and New Jersey, making it so that the load could not be dropped quickly enough. In a desperate attempt, Con Edison began dropping customers from the grid to manually shed the load. Spare a few, save the city. But the city's major power lines were already overtaxed. It was too late. The Ravenswood 3 power generator was the largest generator in New York City. When it went out, it took the entire city with it. And then, blackness.

New York in the summer of 1977 was wildly hot, the city was already broke, and the Son of Sam had already attacked eleven people by the time the lights went out on July 13, and he was still out there. I'm not talking about the lights going out, or the birth of rap music, so much as I'm talking about the kind of landscape in which something frivolous might become political. Looting, rioting, and fires spread throughout the city that night, and there is something to be said about an urgency that arises in the struggling and afraid when what appears to be a basic right is taken away with the snap of a finger.

On the night the lights went out, DJ Grandmaster Caz and his partner Disco Wiz were spinning in a park, with their equipment plugged into a lamppost. They thought they had shorted out all of the city's power themselves. When they realized that they hadn't, Caz found himself among the looters, pulling a mixer out of the store where he had once purchased

DJ equipment. A mixer does a lot of things, but a big thing that it does is allow a wider audience to hear what a DJ is spinning. Rap needed a megaphone, DJs couldn't afford them, and then with darkness came a new kind of wealth.

It must also be mentioned that the birth of hip-hop is pretty much a mythology at this point. And so like all of the best stories told by anyone, anywhere, any part of it could be true or not true. But I like this idea: I like the idea that the lights went out, and on the other side, a genre found new life. I like to imagine that hip-hop became political when someone threw the first rock or brick into a glass door or window and walked inside a store to retrieve a mixer; that hip-hop became political when it took food out of one person's mouth to put food into another's.

By the 1990s, rap had become political to the world but not yet dangerous. Political tones were evident—as in Grandmaster Flash and the Furious Five's "The Message"—but these were more cautionary tales meet neighborhood reportage. Slick Rick's "Children's Story" falls in the same range. These songs and others were political but still felt as though they weren't aiming at a specific target. A target can turn the political into something dangerous.

Who knows how long police have been beating on black folks, but I know some wise heads who will say that as long as there have been police and black skin to bruise, the two have been wed. What I'm saying is that some things just come to you as they have always been and you take them for what they are. Rap came to me as dangerous from the moment in the early 1990s when my parents banned listening to it in our household, and my eldest brother began to sneak tapes into the house.

N.W.A. members were detained by the LAPD for shooting at people with a paintball gun, which is perhaps when rap music became dangerous. While detained, they were taunted and forced to lie facedown in the street, and they had guns pointed at their heads. Real guns, not the paintball gun that one of the group members had in his possession—something that might have gotten them executed on another day, as we have seen played out in my beloved Ohio with the murders of Tamir Rice and John Crawford. But N.W.A. lived, and they went into a studio to record "Fuck Tha Police," their most infamous and notable song.

"Fuck Tha Police" is a song for those who many imagine to be powerless and angry. The thing with N.W.A. was that they knew they weren't powerless. They actually had an acute awareness of their power, particularly in 1988, before the release of their debut album, *Straight Outta Compton*. The group was buzzing and poised to shift the direction of rap, which was then still East Coast dominated. There were rappers from regions other than the East Coast and Northeast, but because of rap's humble beginnings in New York, most of the notable MCs of the era lived east of Ohio. The voice of the West had yet to be fully defined, and the sound certainly hadn't been defined. N.W.A. knew they were setting themselves up to be catalysts, shifting the genre out of its regional clustering.

"Fuck Tha Police" suggests—in part—that people should

rise up violently against this country's police force, and it must be said that nonblack artists have used controversy to sell records for as long as there has been both controversy and a place to sell it. And so yes, underneath some of N.W.A.'s rage and contempt was a marketing plan—one that was partially manufactured by then assistant director of FBI public affairs Milt Ahlerich, who wrote a sprawling letter to their recording company, Priority Records, on the FBI's letterhead addressing the song but never naming it.

"Advocating violence and assault is wrong, and we in the law enforcement community take exception to such action," the letter reads. "Law enforcement officers dedicate their lives to the protection of our citizens, and recordings such as the one from N.W.A. are both discouraging and degrading to these brave, dedicated officers."

When the letter was made public, people set N.W.A. records on fire. Politicians denounced the group and urged parents to keep their children away from the music they made. And not just the music *they* made but also the musical genre they trafficked in. It was the springboard N.W.A. needed to brand themselves as the World's Most Dangerous Group—something that was boosted dramatically when already-hysterical Christians and cops realized that their name stood for "Niggaz Wit Attitudes" the whole time.

And so it can be said that rap became political when the people making it needed it to be fed, and it became dangerous when those people being fed realized they had the power to feed themselves forever off the power they had.

A Tribe Called Quest arrived on the scene at the turn of the decade, in the spring of 1990. The individual members had arrived years earlier. Kamaal Ibn John Fareed and Malik Izaak Taylor grew up together in Queens, New York—childhood friends who used music as a bridge to each other. Before Fareed was Q-Tip, he was MC Love Child, performing occasionally with another pal from Queens Ali Shaheed Muhammad, who acted as his DJ. Before Taylor was Phife Dawg, he was Crush Connection, collaborating with MC Love and Muhammad regularly, before eventually joining their group.

Q-Tip and Ali Shaheed Muhammad went to high school with the group that would become the Jungle Brothers, and on a demo track, Q-Tip opened with a line about being Q-Tip from "a group called quest." Jungle Brothers' member Afrika Baby Bam told him to change it to "A Tribe Called Quest," and so, like all good names, it came from someone else.

While N.W.A. found themselves stirring up hysteria on the West Coast in 1988, in Queens, Q-Tip was being featured for the first time on record, on the Jungle Brothers' song "The Promo"—the final track on their classic 1988 debut album, *Straight Out the Jungle*, which was released exactly three months to the day after N.W.A. released their classic 1988 debut album, *Straight Outta Compton*. These two groups point out the ways that rap artists had begun to craft their own mythologies, like wrestlers in the ring: N.W.A. with their fearless, hyperviolent personas, rooted in some truth but absolutely rooted in some idea of what would make young white people most excited and old white people most afraid; and the Jungle

Brothers, with their heavily Afrocentric imagery, tone, and aesthetic, rooted in some truth but absolutely rooted in some idea of what would make young black people most curious and old black people most welcoming. The turn of the decade is when rap's identity took new and more interesting turns, but it can be argued that the most fascinating spark of it began here: with two albums on two coasts, and two groups laying claim to what they were coming out of.

And within that, there is Q-Tip, on the song "The Promo." He opens with, "My name is Q-Tip from A Tribe Called Quest."

The first single by A Tribe Called Quest was actually "Description of a Fool," though no one ever really heard it until their first album was released, where it was the final song. The first commercial single that A Tribe Called Quest released was a song about losing your wallet. "I Left My Wallet in El Segundo" is an interesting choice for a debut single on its own, made even more interesting by the fact that songs like "Bonita Applebum" and "Can I Kick It?" were also on the album, released as later singles.

El Segundo is a real place—it is a suburban city in Los Angeles County, named El Segundo, Spanish for "The Second" because it was the site of the second Standard Oil refinery in California. El Segundo is also a part of a running gag on the show *Sanford and Son*. The Sanfords lived in Watts, close to El Segundo, and Fred Sanford would often talk his way out of messes by telling wide-ranging stories about something happening in the world around him, with the punch line resting on something absurd happening in El Segundo.

"On the news, there was a Cyclops!" he'd say. "And the Cyclops, he was crying, and he cried into the ocean, and he cried so much that it started a tidal wave in El Segundo!"

And with that, the laugh track would roll.

Q-Tip wrote the title for the song because of Fred Sanford, not because of any affinity to the geography itself. The title came before the song, and therefore, the song had to be built from what the title was asking us to believe.

There are many ways to approach a lead single for a group entering the arena for the first time: you can give the people something that will make you a star, or you can give the people something that best defines who you'll aim to be going forward. If you're lucky, you hit some combination of both. "I Left My Wallet in El Segundo" is definitely the latter of the two options, though it can be said that the single acts as a showcase for the idea that A Tribe Called Quest was going to be driven, largely, by Q-Tip's ambition. He birthed the name, he birthed the title for the first single, and he's the only person performing on the song.

Q-Tip was never interested in a Point-A-to-Point-B perspective as an MC or as a storyteller, so it makes sense that A Tribe Called Quest's first single is a sprawling narrative with an inconsistent narrator telling a story about going on a road trip after his mother left him home alone, and ending up in California after driving from New York for two days. The song's story and lyrics would have one imagine that Q-Tip had perhaps never been to California before, with his branding of it as an entirely desolate wasteland in the middle of nowhere. In the song, Tribe drives through miles of desert before finding a single gas station and a bite to eat. They lament the middle-of-nowhereness of their surroundings, and yet, at the hole-in-the-wall diner they end up in, Q-Tip sees one of the most beautiful women he's ever seen, prompting him to lose his wallet. This is more comically played out in the music video, where all members of Tribe are crammed into a rusted blue Cadillac, looking like a bunch of kids who never expected to be on camera in the first place.

This song shows something about rap and the way rappers on each coast imagined one another and their landscapes at the early turn of the century, before the East Coast–West Coast rap war exploded and so many rappers were confined to their singular bubbles. I don't know for a fact whether or not Q-Tip had ever been to California, but he wrote about it as I imagined it when I was young and living in the landlocked Midwest. Heat and sand, a large and endless sky, a place to get lost, a place to lose things.

The song was quirky and delightful enough for a listener to ignore any glaring plot holes, like the fact that in the story, it takes Q-Tip three days on the road before he realizes that he lost his wallet. By the time of the song's release, rap had already seen its fair share of narrators, chief among them the aforementioned Slick Rick, who wove tales of caution with tales of his own sexual mischief and whimsical, fairy tale–based stories of the world in his head. Hip-hop artists had already cemented themselves as griots, telling stories from their own corner of whatever land they claimed and broadcasting them to a world that might not have access to the interior of that land. If you're N.W.A. or Public Enemy, you want to rattle the cage of public consciousness and push for some uprising among the people to take back what is theirs, or to incite some violence against an oppressor. If you're Too Short, you want to captivate a listening audience of young men who imagined sex but hadn't experienced it beyond their imaginings or the pages of some illicit magazine swiped from the room of a parent or an older sibling.

If you're A Tribe Called Quest, or at least if you're Q-Tip, the story you tell is one that is mundane on the surface, built around something meaningful only to you and a handful of your pals, piled in a car, driving on a stretch of road that seems endless.

People's Instinctive Travels and the Paths of Rhythm is certainly A Tribe Called Quest's debut album, but it could be read entirely as Q-Tip's introduction to the world at large. Q-Tip made the bones of most of the album's production on pause tapes when he was still in high school. The pause tape was something that aspiring producers would dabble in before they had access to proper studio equipment. Back when record stores sold tapes, and dual cassette decks were the norm in most homes, the hopeful producer would play an album and sample from another tape or a record, stopping the tape when the sample finished its rotation. The trick was in the second part, where they would rewind to the beginning of the sample and unpause the tape, which would extend the sample for longer. It was an amateur trick, but it played a huge role in the evolution of rap's sound and the sampling that hip-hop was rooted in. It was akin to the DJ finding the proper groove in a record and flooding a room with drums. Hip-hop's architecture was based on extending the sounds laid by other hands, and the pause tape was an expansion of that. The products of these tapes were often imperfect but good enough to record some vocals over and get a demo tape done. The process was tedious, taking hours of work to perfect and draw several sounds out in sections. It was hip-hop's version of the Wall of Sound, Phil Spector's production technique that involved layering sound over sound to create one cohesive wave of music.

Q-Tip insists that he made the song "Bonita Applebum" first on pause tapes when he was fifteen, and if you listen to the song's components, this would make sense, even when you hear the cleaned-up and sharper version that eventually made it onto *People's Instinctive Travels*. The beat to "Bonita Applebum" consists of five samples.

Appearing first is a sitar riff from the Rotary Connection song "Memory Band" from their 1967 self-titled album. The riff appears in this song sparingly, but Q-Tip stretched it out in "Bonita," peppering the song with it throughout the instrumental.

The next sample is the first part of the song's backbone—the drum beat is built from the beat in Little Feat's "Fool Yourself" from the 1973 album *Dixie Chicken*. In "Bonita," the drums are looped in a sped-up fashion, played back at a pace a bit sharper than Little Feat drummer Richard Hayward played the original.

The second part of the song's backbone comes in the third sample: the breezy, funky keys and guitar from RAMP's "Daylight," from their 1977 album *Come into Knowledge*. This sample is the most important one, because it is the glue that holds all of the others together. When layering sounds in this manner, there has to be a unifying one that each of them can fit into comfortably without throwing the groove off. RAMP's song is both gentle and airy, leaving enough space to be filled by any other chosen noise.

The final two samples operate in the song's ending moments: In Cannonball Adderley's "Soul Virgo," from his quintet's 1970 album *The Price You Got to Pay to Be Free* album, there is a spoken interlude, a voice chanting words like "sex" and "peace." At the end of "Bonita," Q-Tip slows down that voice and uses it as a bridge, with the dying saxophone behind it. This gives way to the closing notes of the song, which bleed into the next song on the album, "Can I Kick It?" The light piano and drum groove was lifted from the Eugene McDaniels song "Jagger the Dagger," which exists briefly before transitioning into the "Walk on the Wild Side" Lou Reed sample that is the major component of "Can I Kick It?"

When laid out this way, it would appear that the art of the sample, in the mind of Q-Tip, was science. He began by laying out pause tapes in his home until 1989, when he had the opportunity to be present for the recording of De La Soul's iconic album *Three Feet High and Rising*. It was in those moments when he was shown around the studio by the in-house recording engineers and afterward was allowed to tinker with all the sampling devices. Seeing his potential and interest, the rapper and producer Large Professor taught him how to use other studio equipment to most effectively hone his sound. Not all young producers have a group of welcoming mentors like Q-Tip had, but not all young producers were as uniquely skilled from their teenage years as Q-Tip was, and not all were as willing as Q-Tip to "dig deep in the crates" to search for sounds. Q-Tip was, in many ways, an extension of rap's early DJs, chipping away at a massive block of music and peeling off only what he needed.

People's Instinctive Travels and the Paths of Rhythm was a far-reaching album that was a new variation on black psychedelia. It wasn't particularly hazy in the way that, say, Hendrix was hazy. But it does feel, instead, like Love's album *Forever Changes* in the way it is utterly unconcerned with anything except for its own vibes and the celebration of them. The album is awash with samples, some of them unfocused and scattered, coming together when least expected. Now, with knowledge of its origins and the mind behind it, people can look back and hear the unpolished excitement in Q-Tip's flights of fancy as a producer. "Public Enemy" is jam-packed with lifted sounds from Luther Ingram and Rufus Thomas and Billy the Baron and his Smokin' Challengers and Malcolm McLaren. "Go Ahead in the Rain" mashes up Jimi Hendrix and "Brother" Jack McDuff while also managing to sneak in a Slave sample. "Push It Along" pairs Grover Washington Jr.'s "Loran's Dance" with "All You Need Is Love" by the Beatles.

It is an album stuffed with a cast of characters, all orchestrated by Q-Tip's vision. Yet he still finds a way to carve himself out as the central force, his somewhat nasally and melodic flow slicing through the tracks with ease. Of all the album's characters, there is one that doesn't find a home as easily.

Phife Dawg is almost an afterthought on *People's Instinctive Travels*. It may not seem like this, because he appears in all of the visuals, and he's present on the album's most popular track, the aforementioned "Can I Kick It?," but beyond that, Phife is only present on three other tracks, or four out of the album's fifteen. The entire group was young—teenagers preparing to enter their twenties—but Phife was the least mature of the bunch, by his own account. He was living at his grandmother's place, running the streets all day and night. Q-Tip wrote all of the lyrics for the album, even the lyrics Phife rapped. Phife stole the show on "Can I Kick It?," but his other verses were largely muted, acting as small bridges to Q-Tip's vocal and instrumental ambition. Phife often had to be dragged to the studio, his stubbornness clashing with Q-Tip's drive and vision. The album was recorded a couple of blocks from Madison Square Garden, at Calliope Studios. Phife would make a brief stop in the studio and then sneak off to Knicks games, leaving Q-Tip and Ali Shaheed Muhammad frustrated but committed to the album's completion, with or without him.

Another part of the story, which speaks to Phife's ambivalence about the project, is the fact that he wasn't signed as an official group member at that point. A Tribe Called Quest was officially only Q-Tip and Ali. Phife and Jarobi were going to start their own group, independent of Tribe, but Jarobi decided to go to culinary school in the middle of this planning, leaving Phife somewhat out in the cold. Tribe welcomed him into the recording sessions and for his contributions to the album, but he wasn't signed to a contract as an official member. It makes sense, then, that he might not be as open to being pushed in the studio in the very particular way that Q-Tip could push people. Because Q-Tip's mind operated at almost unimaginable speeds, his major function was to carry everyone else to his level. The stakes were higher for Q-Tip on this album than they were for Phife, who had no real promise of being signed to the group when the album was complete. Phife was still simply making music with his friends in his spare time, but Q-Tip was trying to build a sound that would carry him for an entire career.

People's Instinctive Travels was critically acclaimed upon its release, though it struggled commercially, taking nearly seven years to achieve gold status. Some of the commercial failing was simply an inability on the part of listeners to understand Q-Tip's sonic vision. When we talk about artists being "ahead of their time," the remarks are often peppered with vague complimentary aspects about some futuristic soundscape sold to an audience that would later come to appreciate it as sounds around them evolved. An example would be something like the frantic and hectic album *Tusk* by Fleetwood Mac, which was a stark departure from the pop-drenched sounds of their previous album, *Rumours*. The album helped signal the New Wave sound, but at the time, it was a confusing release, loved by a few critics but only a fraction as commercially successful as their previous two albums, until the middle of the 1980s, when the sound they were reaching for began to make more and more sense to people.

Q-Tip and A Tribe Called Quest weren't selling futuristic grooves as much as they were selling new interpretations of past grooves, layering samples from every corner of the crates and pulling out only the useful parts of the music. *People's Instinctive Travels* was, indeed, a blueprint for what was to come. Tribe's sound didn't just shift the direction of hip-hop; it offered alternative windows into the world of sampling, cadence, and language. That the album sold better as it aged was simply a reflection of people catching up to it. The mastery in the album was the fact that these were all relatively young artists. Q-Tip was still figuring out how to make the music sound the way he wanted it to sound. And yet, out of all that, he created a stunning, singular debut.

I admit I lost my wallet in another city one time and I did turn back to get it in West Texas, leaving Odessa after reading the book *Friday Night Lights* in some late-teen haze and insisting that I must see the town. The thing about Odessa, Texas, is that it really is a desert. I mean, I'm not saying that there's nothing else there, but I am saying that at one time the town became rich from oil and then the oil left. So you maybe can imagine what I mean when I say that there is a big sky and a lot of land with nothing on it below. That's beauty, though— a kind of America that can make someone feel like the wide-open spaces are calling them and all of that, that is, when not factoring in the people, some of whom wave Confederate flags on their front porches or glare ominously at an unfamiliar black face in a gas station when the person who owns the face puts their wallet on the counter with a bottle of sweet tea and a pack of peanut M&Ms and then gets the hell out of town before anyone else gets too suspicious. And who is to say really why I drove to Odessa, except for the fact that it was summer and I had nothing better to do and I sure didn't have a job or much money except for gas and the occasional road snacks and I wanted to get the hell out of town, and anywhere would have done. Like Q-Tip in his own story, I had the space and freedom and four wheels and a map that pointed me to a place I'd heard of and only imagined. And the thing about road trips is that nothing at the end of the journey can live up to the anticipation of the unseen destination once we arrive there, and so, in my haste to get out of Odessa, I drove an hour or two and reached into my pocket when passing the first fast-food sign I'd seen in miles. And I wish Q-Tip would have gone on to describe the feeling that hits you when you realize you have lost your wallet, or some other precious thing—the way shock begins in your legs and carves a home in your stomach for a while, before even getting to the part of your brain that asks the "What do I do?" question. And I knew I'd left it in the gas station, and I knew I left the gas station in too much of a hurry because once you've seen a harsh look in one too many small towns, you start to get a feeling for what might be on the other end of that look if you stick around too long. And yet, I did a complete U-turn, kicking up sand and dust as I sped back to the gas station, where my wallet was most certainly waiting for me, and the person behind the counter handed it to me without a word, and I got in my old car and headed back east, and the muffler on that car was so loud, but instead of getting it fixed, I just got a louder stereo and I fingered the leather seams of my newly retrieved wallet and I laughed at the absurdity of it all and then I remembered: there's a song for this.

CHAPTER THREE

Push It Along

Let it first be said that it would behoove you to have a crew of
some kind if you are of the wandering sort, or the dancing sort,
or the scrapping sort, or the hustling sort. It would maybe
behoove you to have a crew if you are the rapping sort, but it
is certainly not required. I had a crew first in middle school,
and let it second be said that it is not easy to form a crew. But,
again, it would behoove you to do so, and so you find a crew
out of whatever ashes of coolness you have left after your confidence has been burned to the ground by the rigors of early
teenage life.

My crew was easy to drag out for me. I hung with the kids
who were not entirely uncool but who were also decidedly not
the cool kids. There's a lot of currency in the space between
immensely cool and not at all cool. If they're lucky, a crew can

define coolness on their own terms, because in the larger ecosystem of popularity, they are often forgettable. My crew sometimes wore our clothes backward in the era of Kris Kross, and my crew sometimes pretended not to like sports even though we kind of liked sports. My crew couldn't afford the coolest sneakers on the market, but we could afford ones just cool enough to get by—black ones that could go with any and all of our clothing, some of mine hand-me-down or sewn at home by the hands of my mother or passed down from my older brother, who had them passed down from my oldest brother.

My crew stayed under the radar mostly because we couldn't fight like some of the other crews filling the halls of our school. My brother—a year older—was in a significantly cooler crew, because he could hoop well enough to be respected by the basketball players and he was attractive enough to be desired by the girls. And even though we were from the same home, with similar circumstances and similar genes, he had the confidence to be cool in a way that I didn't. He wore his clothes better, smiled easier, and was generally more appealing to a wider audience of people in our age group. I envied this, of course, even though I found comfort in my crew's relative anonymity. My brother was an actively good person who was also good to be around and good at the things he undertook. I was a significantly less good person who was sometimes fine to be around and marginally good at some of the things I undertook. I say this to say that having my brother be who he was at our school and having me be who I was at our school seems like it would be awful on its face, but it added to the general idea of anonymity as a function of my ability to thrive.

It's not as if my brother didn't claim me or acted ashamed of my presence in school. It's just that when he was around, his presence rendered me somewhat invisible. I realized this early on, and instead of fighting against it, I found some comfort in it. I didn't have to live up to the expectations of anything except for silence.

Once, when he was in the eighth grade, my brother's crew got into a fight with some other crew. By this I mean nothing in the realm of gang violence. I do mean that one group of friends rubbed another group of friends the wrong way, and before you knew it, fists were being thrown in a field, and my brother charged into the fray. The fight was the scandal of that particular middle school year. The boy who was beaten up the most was white, and most of his assailants were black. The optics of the fight were difficult for parents to handle, and the violence seemed to be a stark uptick from the occasional scuffle that was often quickly broken up in the school hallway after some circling and yelling in faces.

My parents didn't understand my brother's involvement in the fight, or maybe they did but they had to be parents—showing remorse for the hurt boy and contempt for those who hurt him, even (or perhaps especially) if they were raising one of the perpetrators. Though I do expect and believe that my parents once also had a crew and they knew the inner workings of what it was to have a crew, there is still a line that gets crossed when blood ends up on someone's asphalt. I have no hard evidence on the distance between a crew and a gang, or what makes someone designate one group a crew and another a gang. I imagine it might depend on who owns the eyes looking upon the cluster of people considering themselves a crew, and what skin is most prominent on that cluster of people, and perhaps the clothing they have on—how it hangs or doesn't hang from their bodies.

I also imagine that there is something to be said about violence, and how it manifests itself in crews or doesn't. I can't speak for the concern of my parents, but I imagine that a small part of it had to do with the fact that a group of boys had inflicted violence on another group of boys, and this was in the 1990s, when gang hysteria was at its peak in our neighborhood and in our school. Some of the hysteria can be attributed to that, but some of it was firmly rooted in what was playing out in the neighborhood: boys who were young and impressionable were being pulled into gangs as a way of forming their own communities.

The difference between a gang and a crew sometimes boils down to reputation or intention. My crew was not preoccupied with appearances, and neither was my brother's, but the point I'm making is that sometimes you run into the fray in the name of people you love, even if you don't share blood with them. And that might make you a gang or a crew, depending on who is assessing the fray, or who is defining the kind of love that might make one throw a fist on behalf of another.

My crew didn't throw fists, though I'd like to think we would have scrapped for each other if need be. We cracked jokes at a high rate, and that's what kept us sharp. Like Phife Dawg, we were small and of dark skin, and we knew that our wit could be weaponized in tense moments. If cornered in a hallway, for example, we might be clever enough to briefly win over the heart of a bully by cracking jokes at the expense of someone lower on the spectrum of popularity than we were. This, again, is why we existed at what appeared to be the best intersection: the place where there is someone below you that you could turn to and lay a joke on in order to escape what might be a more physically painful fate for yourself. I am, of course, not advocating for this chain of command now, as an adult. But the primary language around having a crew or being a crew also had to do with survival.

By all accounts, me and my boys were nerds, but we were acceptable nerds. We were kind of ahead of our time in this way, though it is laughable to try and sell that now, as I'm sure you know. But there is an age where that became cool, and an age where it still appears to be cool now—one where black people age into some kind of alternativeness that allows for a celebration of simply doing nothing but appearing smart or interesting or witty. If nothing else, my boys and I were tuned in to popular culture in a way that many of our more popular peers simply weren't at the time. Some of them were going out at night with other cool kids from other schools, and some of them were on sports teams, or some were simply reveling in the type of teenage debauchery that makes memories for adulthood. My crew and crews like mine were at home, watching sitcoms and cartoons, or dubbing tapes from the radio. This, too, was a feature of survival. We weren't cool, but people would come to us to find out what *was* cool. To that end, we had a purpose. To have a purpose was to be needed, and to be needed was to be slightly protected. I would ride the back of the school bus with headphones on, attached to my Walkman, and people would talk to me because they knew I was listening to good music, and they'd want to know what music was good so that they could talk about it in their far cooler circles.

If nothing else, me and my crew of weirdos understood our way around a soundtrack.

If you were of the rapping sort in the 1990s, it would definitely behoove you to have a crew, and everyone had a crew, so if nothing else, having a crew just meant you weren't left out. After the respective successes of the Jungle Brothers' *Straight Out the Jungle* in 1988, De La Soul's *Three Feet High and Rising* in 1989, and A Tribe Called Quest's *People's Instinctive Travels and the Paths of Rhythm* in 1990, rap music had an interesting assortment of sounds on its hands. The sounds on the albums weren't too drastic of a departure from East Coast rap's percussion-based sounds, but the evolution in each album was reaching toward something new and refreshing, so that by the time Tribe's album dropped, there was a clear and direct lineage mapped through each album released to that point.

A pivotal point in the history of the Native Tongues collective is the song "Buddy," which appeared as the eighteenth track on the sprawling *Three Feet High and Rising*. The song, produced by Prince Paul, provided the rap world with what would eventually come to be known as the first Native Tongues collaboration. The De La Soul song also featured Jungle Brothers, Monie Love, and the first notable guest verse by Q-Tip. De La Soul and Jungle Brothers had previously met at a show in Boston, and they linked up for the recording of the song shortly thereafter. At one point during the recording, Q-Tip was summoned to the studio at some time past midnight. The video was drenched in Afrocentric garb and also turned into a comical dance party, with the members of De La Soul riding about town on scooters. It was a ridiculous but fun venture that acted as an introduction for what was to come.

De La Soul and the Jungle Brothers were something like older siblings to A Tribe Called Quest, the younger and sometimes irresponsible brothers who were not yet as able to channel their fun and quirky-but-righteous concepts into polished products the way Jungle Brothers and De La Soul did. The idea was that *People's Instinctive Travels* was a fun album made by kids who got a blueprint from their older, cooler pals—if not older by age, then older by experience. This initial run of Native Tongues albums that existed before the collective had even named themselves presents a fascinating glimpse into a moment in time. Crews and collectives had existed in rap well before Native Tongues—rap itself was founded on the pillars of collectives. The Universal Zulu Nation was started by Afrika Bambaataa in 1974, its bones formed by reformed gang members, who, together, were looking to organize events for young people in the Bronx that combined music and dance and art, pulling together some of hip-hop's original elements. Zulu Nation didn't have a consistent run of members, but it did lay the groundwork for the idea of crews taking on the world of hip-hop as a unified force. The Rock Steady Crew rose to prominence in the late 1970s, gaining notoriety for their breaking and dancing performances, first in the Bronx and then later in Manhattan. A group of six teenagers from the Harlem projects formed and called themselves the Crash Crew, one of the first groups of MCs to be recorded in 1980, when they dropped the song "High Power Rap" under the name Disco Dave and the Force of the Five MCs. Later, there was the infamous Juice Crew, consisting of mostly Queens rap artists in the mid-1980s: Kool G Rap, Big Daddy Kane, Marley Marl, Biz Markie, MC Shan, and Roxanne Shanté, to name a few. To some extent, hip-hop's entire legacy revolved around finding a group of your people and taking on whatever the world had to offer with them at your side. So by the early 1990s, still at the height of the collective era, A Tribe Called Quest knew they needed a bigger group.

The core members of Native Tongues were the Jungle Brothers, De La Soul, and a fully formed Tribe Called Quest—with Phife and Jarobi locked in to complete the group. Other members considered part of the original core group were Monie Love, Queen Latifah, the group Black Sheep, a group of young rappers called Leaders of the New School—which featured a charismatic young MC named Busta Rhymes, French MC Lucien Revolucien, upstart group Fu-Schnickens, and a sixteen-year-old rapper named Chi-Ali.

The musical breadth of the group was wide, which made Native Tongues more fascinating than any other rap collective before them. They were only loosely tethered, by a set of imagined and always-shifting ideals. Afrocentrism, sure. But the idea of Afrocentrism within the collective was a rapidly changing thing. The Jungle Brothers would wear the massive black leather medallions, sewn together with a red, black, and green Africa in the direct center. This was a fashion staple for a very particular kind of black person in the early 1990s. My oldest brother would wear them to school, and I'd see them in corner stores on the block, selling for $10 a pop. The idea was eschewing the gold jewelry so prevalent in rap at the time and getting back to their idea of what their roots were. In the early nineties, Queen Latifah wore kente cloth prints, and sometimes animal prints, and sometimes crowns atop her head.

While the gender politics in Native Tongues were fairly progressive for the time they existed in, it could be argued that Latifah's 1989 album *All Hail the Queen* is the most forward-facing Native Tongues release of them all from the standpoint of lyricism and content. For as invested in Afrocentrism and a free-flowing brand of spiritual uplift as they were, Native Tongues was still largely a boy's club. Latifah—and later her protégé Monie Love—upset that concept in different ways: Latifah was interested in turning a lens toward the layers and complexities of black womanhood. It would be reductive to paint Latifah as a matriarch in contrast to the skilled and rambunctious group of young men making up the rest of Native Tongues. To be aware that your presence in a space is political is to sometimes assume and take on the responsibilities that come with that presence, whether or not you feel as though you should have to. Though they existed in an era when women were more prominent on the mic than in any other era of hip-hop, Latifah and Monie Love, being the only women in the collective, didn't allow themselves to shrink from what their presence as respected peers among a group of exciting young rappers gave them an opportunity to do. Latifah was a particularly skilled and feared MC—*All Hail the Queen* was critically acclaimed in part for Latifah's ability to rap circles around her guests on the album, including De La Soul and KRS-One. Yes, there were feminist politics on the album, but Latifah's greatest act was her ability to lyrically ascend not just to the level of her direct male peers but above their level, and to do it effortlessly.

The album's most lasting cut is the track "Ladies First," which introduced the rap world to Simone Johnson, a UK rapper who started in the British rap crew known as Jus Bad, before branching out on her own as Monie Love. Love's debut album, *Down to Earth*, was released a year after Latifah's in 1990. The album also had the in-house Native Tongues sound, produced by Afrika Baby Bam of the Jungle Brothers. Love was also a skilled MC, but she utilized her skill set differently from Latifah. She was more of a romantic—a hippie in a twenty-year-old body. Her music was saturated with a very specific type of joy and freedom, her album cover speckled with flowers. Her biggest hit was "It's a Shame (My Sister)," which garnered her a Grammy nomination. The song is a cautionary tale about a woman in an abusive relationship, which cemented Love as a rigorous and detailed storytelling MC, like fellow UK MC Slick Rick. But beneath that single, Love was far more interested in partying in innocent fashion, digging through old poetry, and dancing than in writing tales of despair and abuse. She didn't run counter to Latifah in this way; she was interested in the type of uplift that sisterhood could find at the house party.

Native Tongues allowed themselves to be fleshed out in this way: there was a character or a personality for everyone. Dres and Mista Lawnge made up Black Sheep, a vehicle that allowed Dres to escape a life that had landed him in prison during his not-so-distant past. For them, Afrocentrism was about defining your way out of anywhere that kept you confined.

The Leaders of the New School were teenagers at the time of their first album's release, rapping on *A Future Without a Past* about P.T.A. scandals, teacher drama, lunchroom and after-school shenanigans. They predated the idea of "carefree black youth" that we often see now attached to black youth running through streets or diving into pools of cool water or living when a young black child elsewhere has died. But Leaders of the New School embodied that. Most of the Native Tongues were fairly young at the time of their inception, but not all of them wore their youth boldly and unapologetically. Leaders of the New School were kind of proudly immature and comfortable in their raucous playfulness. The group consisted of Dinco D and Charlie Brown, who were skilled enough but were largely acting as a vehicle for the talented, wildly animated, and consistently show-stealing Busta Rhymes, who was eighteen at the time of the album's release. Leaders of the New School lasted just two albums, but—particularly on their debut album—they provided an insight into a youthful absurdity that some of the younger Native Tongues fans could attach themselves to.

And speaking of youth, it was Chi-Ali I found myself most fascinated by at the time. Ali was the youngest member of the Native Tongues, at only fifteen years of age when the collective came to life. He was also the most fashion-forward, as one might expect a teenager still in high school to be. He wore

Cross Colours, the fashion trend of the moment; large sweaters with names of historically black colleges on them; baggy jeans with Nike tennis shoes. While so many of the other Native Tongues were interested in distancing themselves from the mainstream projections of hip-hop and blackness, Chi-Ali was immersing himself in them. He was also interesting because he seemed to take pleasure in both his status as the collective's little brother and his ability to rhyme about topics that, for him, seemed mature. A few years after his decline, a close comparison to his role in the Tongues would be Shyheim, who was the boy wonder of the Wu-Tang Clan, often on the outside looking in but valuable for a topical dexterity that belied his age. Chi-Ali was a precursor to that, with his album *The Fabulous Chi-Ali* being released in 1992 when he was sixteen, featuring production from Mista Lawnge and guest verses from Phife, Dres, Trugoy, and Fashion on the song "Let the Horns Blow." Chi-Ali's age was unmistakable in his wavering, sometimes cracking voice. But, unlike Leaders of the New School, his topical range went beyond tales of school and teenage debauchery. He rapped about sex and romance, violence and fantasies of violence, and material wealth. As far as bad boys went, Chi-Ali was the bad boy of Native Tongues merely by drifting slightly from the path of his older counterparts. He was the edgier glimpse of youth, a kid who grew up on a slightly rougher end of the tracks and had the mind and language with which to make that plain. At one point, he felt to some like the most promising member of Native Tongues, not just because of his youth, but because of the wide range he could traverse almost seamlessly. He was the offshoot of what

Native Tongues aspired to be: young people making music with each other, hoping to feed off of each other's strengths. Chi-Ali was as sharp and fearless as Queen Latifah, as clever as Q-Tip, as fashion-forward and streetwise as Phife and Dres. It seemed as if he was the most likely to sustain a long and adventurous career.

I will spoil the story here and say that like all great things in music and beyond, the Native Tongues were short lived as a fully formed idea. Of course, the collaborations continue to this day, largely between De La Soul and Q-Tip. But the collective itself began to derail around 1993, less than three years into its run. It was difficult for the members to maintain a path toward each other with careers and levels of popularity reaching different heights for each. The 1993 Jungle Brothers album *J Beez wit the Remedy* faltered after running into significant release delays with their label. By 1993, A Tribe Called Quest had released *Midnight Marauders*, the crown jewel of the Native Tongues albums, which also broke them out of the Native Tongues sound and ethos and into the larger world beyond. De La Soul had released *Buhloone Mindstate*, which was only a small sonic departure from their earlier work instrumentally, but lyrically, on the track "In the Woods," Posdnuos made the group's intentions clear with a simple line:

"Yo that native shit is dead."

For the Native Tongues, there was no loud and messy breakup that echoed for years after. There was just a kind of quiet dislodging that—given the continued careers of most of the collective—would have gone unnoticed if not for the sheer lack of collaborative efforts that followed 1993. That was the year the collective found themselves moving in different directions. Queen Latifah—who by then had enjoyed small roles in the films *Jungle Fever* and *House Party 2*—signed on to a show called *Living Single*, a sitcom about the lives of four black women. The show was a hit, enjoying a five-year run, during which Latifah also starred in major feature films like *Set It Off* and *Hoodlum*. After the early success of three great albums, Latifah didn't release new music from 1993 until 1998. Leaders of the New School put out a lackluster album in 1993, *T.I.M.E.*, which charted above their first but wasn't nearly as critically acclaimed; most listeners by that time were only tuning in for Busta Rhymes and no one else. In an infamous clip, the group was seen arguing in an appearance on *Yo! MTV Raps* in the fall of 1993, with Busta Rhymes and Charlie Brown having an intense conversation about Busta stealing the show from the rest of the members. It was a rare thing, to watch a group of young and promising rappers disband right in front of an audience's eyes. The group made it official shortly thereafter, and Busta Rhymes went on to individual success in 1996 with his debut album, *The Coming*. Monie Love's second album was also released in 1993, titled *In a Word or 2*. It featured production by Prince on a song called "Born 2 B.R.E.E.D.," which was an acronym for "Build Relationships where Education and Enlightenment Dominate." The song was a minor chart success, peaking at number eighty-nine on the Billboard Hot 100. Love's second album, though much like her first, didn't show enough growth for people to remain excited about her, and it crept away with a whisper, as did her career, until she resurfaced several years later as a radio DJ. After hitting gold with their 1991 debut album, *A Wolf in Sheep's Clothing*, boosted by the single "The Choice Is Yours," Black Sheep released their second album, *Non-Fiction*, in 1994. With very little promotion or label interest, particularly after the Native Tongues hype had all but died down, the album fell by the wayside and became instantly forgettable. The group disbanded shortly thereafter. "The Choice Is Yours" plays in car commercials sometimes, and I hear it when I'm out with pals, but when I ask them if they remember Black Sheep, no one does. But they know all the words to the song.

The case of Chi-Ali is both confusing and heartbreaking. After the moderate success of *The Fabulous Chi-Ali*, he largely vanished from hip-hop altogether, without a sound. At the end of the 1990s, he made an appearance on Dres's solo album *Sure Shot Redemption*, offering a short verse in the song "It's Going Down." And then he disappeared again.

He resurfaced in January of 2000, when he shot and killed Sean Raymond during an argument in the Bronx. Raymond was the brother of Chi-Ali's daughter's mother. Raymond was staying with Chi-Ali and his family, while Chi was hustling, selling drugs to support his new family. Once Chi and his daughter's mother fell out, he moved to Harlem. About a year later, there was an altercation between his baby's mother and her brother, and Chi was summoned with a phone call that escalated into an argument over money and drugs, which got tense. Chi went to the corner where he knew Raymond would be hustling. The dispute became heated. Chi carried a gun with him to the block, as he often did. He pulled it out and shot Raymond twice before running away and throwing the gun in the water. He spent over a year on the run, first in Atlanta, and then bouncing around various East Coast cities. His friends held him down, or he would hustle in places where he knew he'd be safe. He stayed south of New York, selling drugs and committing small robberies. He hit *America's Most Wanted* in late 2000, and then again in early 2001. In March, he made the mistake of returning to New York City. He was staying with a friend when police banged on the door, and I imagine that he was perhaps too worn down to run anymore. Being a fugitive can be exhausting, particularly with safe havens dwindling and with no crew to hold you up.

There is a clip I love of Chi-Ali on *Yo! MTV Raps* from 1993, when the Native Tongues were crumbling, but his career still seemed like a promising one that could lift itself up from their ashes. It's a simple promo clip, maybe thirty-five seconds long. Chi is in a leather bomber jacket too big for his small frame. He kicks a brief freestyle. His voice cracks in the middle of it, and he flashes a confident sneer when it ends: the youngest Native Tongue, left to his own devices, with seemingly endless potential.

The thing about Native Tongues is that they were like my crew, or potentially your crew. They were uncool enough to define a new type of cool on their own terms. They were successful, but not entirely always what the popular kids were listening to. They fashioned themselves as outsiders, and the thing about fashioning yourself as an outsider is that no one can call you anything that you haven't already decided for yourself. The Native Tongues briefly built a world in which they knew themselves as each other's people. The collective is, more that anything, a support system. Musically, yes. But beyond that, it is a grouping of friends telling each other that their ideas are valuable, that someone will believe in them, even if the people who believe in them are confined to the same studio, tinkering in all of the same weird ways. There is a sadness there—from a knowledge that nothing as pure and self-mythologized as that can last. The worlds most at risk of collapsing are the ones we pull together ourselves, out of thin air, or thin ideas, but with dear friends.

A Tribe Called Quest outgrew the Native Tongues quicker than anyone else. Arguably, Q-Tip's vision outpaced any reasonable future the collective could have had together. Beyond that, it was a question of ambition. Not everyone wanted to act, or DJ. A Tribe Called Quest wanted to make as many classic records as they could. Sound and style are fleeting in hip-hop—more so now than they were then—but there was an urgency to Q-Tip and Tribe's approach. They wanted to run fully into the moment while they still had one to run into. The joy of collectivism aside, there was a process that had to be catered to.

I miss loosely defined collectives in rap music, and I think the genre misses them, too. They aren't entirely obsolete, though. The Los Angeles collective Odd Future, formed by Tyler, the Creator in 2007, is unlike Native Tongues in sound but similar in spirit: a bunch of young, talented artists, tethering themselves together for the sake of community or collaboration, or just from the desire to be weird together. So many crews now are tied together by the same record label, which makes things difficult when the business end of things begins to fall apart. Cash Money Records has gone through so many iterations, with only Lil Wayne remaining as a core functioning member, it's hard to consider them a crew. When hard business is involved—I mean when one member's business directly affects whether or not you will be consistently paid—it's difficult to put that into the context of a crew, who are just looking to one another for creative lighthouses or for some emotional respite from a grueling industry. The songs begin to sound like they have checks being chased at the end of every hook.

In the mid to late 1990s, a new era of rappers and producers took up the Native Tongues mantle, like a group of super-heroes, subbing into the old, dormant costumes of their departed elders: Common, J Dilla, Mos Def, The Pharcyde. It was cool in name only. The new class didn't collaborate nearly as much, beyond J Dilla providing soundtracks for several of them. This group didn't have the same free-flowing spirit of the first collective. Rather, it was a band of artists trying to lift a flag but being worn down by its weight before the wind could catch it.

Still, I understood it and valued it from my small corner of the world. I know what it is to have heroes and want to slide a foot into their shoes, whether or not the fit is perfect. I know what it is to walk into a world that seems wild and eager to swallow you whole and want someone at your side, even if they are at your side in name only and nothing else. There is plenty out there worth doing alone, but for everything else, there is a need for your people. It would behoove you to have a crew.

CHAPTER FOUR

The Low End

DEAR TIP,

I, too, have in interest in that which can be felt more than heard. You know this from jazz, as I do, but also from the way the body reacts with a low, joyful moan after placing the first bite of a good meal on your tongue. I'm talking about vibrations. In music, it works best if one imagines hearing as a straight line, with the larger number of hertz on the high end and the smaller number of hertz on the low end. Any music you hear falls along that spectrum. Higher noises—like cymbals crashing together or a car stereo with the treble turned all the way up—fall on the high end. Sounds that demand the ear's most eager attention. Sounds that are jarring enough to get a room to snap to focus. On the extreme end of this spectrum would be some guitar feedback, wrung through a speaker.

The low end is where the bass and the kick drums exist. You found a home here, as I did listening to the bass licks of Ron Carter and Stanley Clarke on good speakers and feeling my chest rattle a little bit with each slow walk of the fingers along a string. Tip, what I most love about "Jazz" is the way the *Low End* is not only desired but prayed to. I am wondering what space you went to when you let your chest direct your musical curiosities and allowed your ears to rest. Some might say it is too wild to strip away all those sounds and just leave a song's backbone, but you knew what you were trying to spell out: an homage to the horns and strings—bowing to Ron Carter himself and promising not to curse too much on the record if he came in and played some bass for you.

Jive Records never knew what they had, and I know you understood this always, but it's a good time to say it again now. They didn't deserve the album, but you gave it to them anyway. When asked about the sophomore slump, you said, "What the fuck is that? I'm going to make *The Low End Theory*." And I must say that I am impressed by how you never imagined a failure at your doorstep. Maybe the idea was that if you never left the studio after making the first album, there was no true sophomore album—just a continuation, another arm attached to the body you were building.

It is really something to make the music talk so that the rapper doesn't have to speak until they are ready. I love the sample as you love the sample, Tip—for how it can be extracted from the past and stretched over a sound reaching for the future. On "Check the Rhime," there was Grover Washington Jr. again, as he was in 1975, when he put out back-to-back albums that were both critical and commercial darlings, one in the winter and one in the summer. I loved the way you stripped his tune "Hydra" down to its base elements and let it rattle around a bit along the spine of "Check the Rhime," but not so much that it drowns out the Minnie Riperton sample. I love the deep and chunky guitar plucks from "Baby, This Love I Have." I, too, have dug in the crates and found that record: *Adventures in Paradise*, the record that came after the album that made Minnie a household name. This is also a type of sophomore record, isn't it? "Baby, This Love I Have" is a perfect album opener—a reintroduction, if you will. Maybe all the samples you chose were chosen by way of reintroduction, as you imagined your own sound being reintroduced.

Don't you love the cover of *Adventures in Paradise*? Minnie, propped up on a chair with a real lion at rest beside her. The story I've heard goes that there were two lions at first, but the initial lion snapped at Riperton and attacked her without warning. The lion's handler removed the first lion and brought in the second. The second, upon seeing Riperton, laid right down next to her and didn't move. Shortly after the album cover was shot, she found out she had cancer and was given six months to live. She made it longer than that, but I've been thinking about how the art of the sample is also the art of breathing life into someone who doesn't have a life anymore. And I say this and know that you are not in the business of resurrection as much as you are in the business of feeling, but I hate that Minnie Riperton was lost before I could live at the same time as she lived, and I hate that she is only known for the one song and nothing more, and I hate that I cannot hear that song and think that she sang it without knowing how much longer she was going to live.

But I suppose none of us truly know, Tip. Which is why the sample is a joy, isn't it? The wind blows a memory of someone into a room through sound, and the architect captures that memory with their bare hands and puts it on wax. Is this, too, the low end? The feeling of something familiar that sits so deep in your chest that you have to hum it out? The James Brown on "Show Business" or the Sly Stone sample on "Jazz." There are cookouts and *Soul Train* lines on this album. There are hot rooms and hot card games. I imagine the low end to be anything you could touch once but is now just a fading dream. I imagine the low end to be a bassline that rattles your teeth, too. But I also consider the low end to be the smell of someone you once loved coming back to you. Someone who sang along to Aretha, or Minnie, or Otis. Someone who loved you once and then loved nothing.

PHIFE DAWG,

It was a bad one for the Knicks last season, I know. The problem with a team like that is that they're just good enough to give you hope, but not good enough to fulfill that hope. I like John Starks, even when he shoots too much, or even when he's a bit of a menace on the court. He's tough to handle and tough to deal with. But the payoff happens, eventually. It comes in bursts, sure. But it happens. You can tell he annoys Patrick Ewing. Everyone knows Starks is going to be big eventually. His

7.6 points per game don't feel like much, especially when he is shooting 29 percent of his three-pointers. But I like a guy who isn't afraid to shoot a team out of a game, because it means he'll eventually shoot them into some games, you know? Someone who isn't afraid to miss is surely also not afraid to get hot and stay hot. Sure, if you're the Knicks, you hitch your star on Patrick Ewing and let him carry you as far as he can. You bank on Charles Oakley's defense and reliable rebounding. But you need a player like John Starks. Every team needs an enigma, or a player that makes someone throw something across a room one minute and cheer their name the next.

What I like about Starks is that he's willing to fight. He got kicked outta college for stealing some kid's stereo equipment. Then he went to another college and got kicked out for smoking weed in his dorm room and listening to rap. He worked at a grocery store while averaging eleven points per game at one college, and then went to another. He didn't even get drafted. Had to work his way up to the NBA through the minor leagues, where they pay you next to nothing. And now, here he is. He's the quintessential New York player. He has the city's architecture built directly into his style of play. He endures, and it isn't romantic. It's peppered with drugs and theft and jail time. But if there's a fight to be had, you want him next to you.

Phife, I love Starks as I love you, perhaps because both of you strike me as people I would want by my side if something were to go down that I didn't know if I could find my way out of. Some might think that the message underneath all of this is that Q-Tip is Ewing, the fearless and stable leader, and you are Starks, the unpredictable but brilliant sidekick. But I think what makes the most sense to me is that you are both equals, fighting for your own space in relation to each other. Perhaps Tip is Ewing, but Ewing found himself needing Starks to thrive and survive more than he could on his own. This is what made your dynamic worth celebrating.

I am glad for the story I read. The one where, when exiting a train, you ran into Q-Tip by chance, after having not spoken to him for some months after finishing work and touring on *People's Instinctive Travels*. It's funny how chance encounters work, I suppose. When you were both ready to find the way to each other again, the journey began.

Let me first say that I know you were but a whisper on the first album, but also, where would it be without your energy? Where would it be without your introduction to rap, the idea that you had arrived and were unlike anything before you? I appreciate stability so that I might appreciate that which shakes up stability, and I felt this on "Push It Along" in just a few bars. It's what you feel when John Starks checks into a game: the idea that everything that happened before is about to be altered.

Tip is the conservative but skilled MC, in the way that Ewing was the reliable, back-to-the-basket center who would bully down low with technical grace to get his buckets. You, though. What you did was an act of brilliance, flying in from nowhere, a rush of colors behind you, throwing up everything like you've never missed before. This is how you came alive on *The Low End Theory*, a whole album about love and loss and fear and rage. I get it. Maybe *People's Instinctive Travels* wasn't the thing you had a taste for. It all seemed like some trick that would never pan out. But on *The Low End Theory*, you decided to get serious. You started writing more, like a writer's writer. I heard it in the way your punch lines began to leap off the page, or in the unexpected angles they began to take. I laughed with you in awe. It is great to have a group with one feared MC, and you made it so Tribe had two.

The Knicks will maybe never get past the Bulls, Phife, and I'm sure you know this. I'm hoping that you'll make some peace with this. It's a question of era, really. There is nothing like playing a game as well as you can and having it still not be good enough because there are titans roaming your land.

But this makes me wonder, what did it feel like not to know what that was? To be the titans roaming the landscape, if for just a short while. Maybe you don't give a shit about basslines or sound frequencies or how low the human ear can hear. Maybe you don't care about the way a good bass kick can briefly stop the heart before it starts again, refreshed. The right speaker makes the body a quick ghost before kicking it back to life, and I find that fascinating, and if you don't, that's fine. I guess I can't expect you to do much but show up and do what you imagine your job is. Shaking the table. Rapping better than anyone else in the room.

TIP,

The police showed us what the body of Rodney King could take, didn't they? On the concrete of Los Angeles, the batons cut through the air and then fell again on King's writhing body.

It is hard to tell what could bring this specific type of ferocity out of anyone—particularly those who insist on serving and protecting. Yes, Rodney King was drunk, and had led police on a high-speed chase through the L.A. streets while behind the wheel of a Hyundai. I don't know what measure of reckless-ness warrants a type of anger that results in what Rodney King got, but the American public got Rodney King.

It must be an odd life, to be introduced to the world first through your flaws and then through your blood on the ground, or your swollen face in a mug shot, or your bent body in a wheelchair. It is said that King patted the back of his pants when exiting the vehicle, which made police believe he had a weapon. I've been thinking a lot about invisible weapons and how they relate to the body itself. I have nothing on me, but in the wrong neighborhood, I have everything on me. And it's as simple as a move for a pocket, or a low whistle in the wrong direction, or the song spilling out of my rolled-down car windows.

Los Angeles wasn't on fire yet when *The Low End Theory* was being made or when it was released. But it would be on fire by the time the songs were playing in heavy rotation all across America. What had already begun, though, were all of the replays of Rodney King's beating, his legs twitching on the ground with each strike of the baton. The constant replaying of the footage was laying a new groundwork for rage in com-munities miles away.

I first watched it in the dark of a living room with my par-ents, who often had the news on. I remember my father's silence and that is about it. I was too young to know how to feel.

But I do wonder where the visuals arrived first for you, Tip. If you sat, with your hands shaking, or if you covered your eyes with each blow. You knew already. The police in Queens would hassle you enough for you to understand that they could, if they wanted to, do harm and get away with it.

I understand more clearly now what I didn't understand then: how *The Low End Theory* isn't only about that which cannot be heard, but it is also about society's unseen, the people who exist but may be able to navigate an entire landscape as invisible, until some violence or some tragedy deems them less so. The downtrodden, yes. But also those who are getting by, just trying to make a chain of solid days out of a mess of a year or a wreck of a lifetime, who need a way out but don't know where the windows are—the people living very normal lives until they are the target of something greater than themselves.

Maybe it was always time to make a political album anyway, wasn't it? Maybe what N.W.A. was trying to chip away at was right there all along, but you guys were never ones to point two middle fingers in the direction of your foes. You were never the sonic force that Public Enemy was, with a big-voiced siren shouting down the kingdom of your oppressors until their empire trembled to dust.

What is political in a country that would leave you bleeding on the concrete? What is political when those who did the beating walk free of all charges, despite the footage of their crime? I don't know if you have to answer that, Tip. But *The Low End Theory* at least has characters at the heart of these questions. I most love Miss Elaine from "Everything Is Fair." Do you love

Van Morrison as I do, Tip? On a night of your choosing, I could play the song "Madame George" for you, and we might sit together and talk about all of the ways you bring to life a character in the same manner that Van Morrison brought to life a character: Madame George down on Cyprus Avenue, whom Morrison looks upon with curiosity and compassion in equal measure. I like to close my eyes while listening to "Everything Is Fair" and imagine that you perhaps stumbled upon *Astral Weeks* in one of your many record store excursions and skipped straight to "Madame George," listening to the way Van Morrison wrote a listener into some small dose of empathy.

Miss Elaine hustles weed and manages to get by without the cops hassling her. You wrote of longing for her, maybe not even entirely out of romance, but out of a love for power. You write of getting close to her and then her turning around and trusting you to sell her drug. She gave into your advances but then pulled away. And you write of how she kept the gun closer than any person and became consumed by dealing. It's a love story, maybe. But it's mostly a narrative on what one must do to survive in a city. What it is to be loved by the streets more than you can ever imagine being loved by a person. I want to imagine this as political because it is a song about the varied ways we all survive. In the song, you sold drugs because you desired closeness, and I imagine that, too, is a type of hustle. We do whatever we must to get closer to the people we desire. This is also the low end, the dark and endless humming of want, which opens the door and beckons us to all manner of ills.

I thank you for knowing the type of political album that the world needed at the time: one that wrapped its politics in ideas of a type of freedom. "Do your ill dance, don't think about the next man." Thank you for showing us how we might, if we are lucky, be able to dance our way into a type of brief forgetting. Let the other groups have the anger. They knew how to navigate it better than you all ever did. I know what it is to watch a man beaten on the ground and shout with rage. I know you know that as well as I do. But I also know what it is to fashion that rage into a hunt for empathy, even among people who likely have none. And if all else fails, at least there will be something left for our people to move their hips to.

PHIFE,

I didn't learn until years after I first heard it that you had to fight with Tip to make "Butter" yours and yours alone. I don't know how else the song would work. The way the Weather Report sample floated onto the track and laid itself out made sense for you and only you. The Weather Report song is "Young and Fine," and it has no language, but for the way the horns dance in and out of each other's paths as a conversation, which I admire. But you are under no obligation to admire yourself. I also admire the way the bass barges into the song as an unwanted dweller who becomes the life of the party. I love Jaco Pastorius for the same reasons I love John Starks, I guess. It's the thing about knowing a fighter when you see one.

It killed Jaco, so it wasn't all good. After shows, he would start bar fights and let his ass get kicked. For the thrill of it, he said. In 1987, he got kicked out of a Carlos Santana concert and then walked into some bar in Florida, broke through a glass door, and started a fight with a bouncer, who beat him to his eventual death. So I guess not all fighters know when to call it quits and stick to what they're good at. But in the moment, when the balance is found, there can be brief and unforgettable magic.

I'm glad you fought for "Butter," because it is the song on *The Low End Theory* that most made it clear to me that you were now a member of the group, there to stay and flourishing, unable to be pulled away by the streets or your many distractions and passions.

You are of a different brand of storyteller than your partner Tip, and I always loved the lens through which you placed yourself directly at the center of a story, not sparing yourself for the sake of narrative. "Butter" is the song where you were at your best, doing that thing where you are half confident and half afraid. Comical, but taking the jokes out on your own body first. It's dense and sprawling—a ride worth grasping on to. The crescendo, in which we figure out that you haven't learned your lesson, goes like this:

> *You wanna be treated right, see Father MC*
> *Or check Ralph Tresvant, for sensitivity*
> *'Cause I am not the one, I got more game than Parker*
> *   Brothers*
> *Phife Dawg is on the mic and I'm smooth like butter*

What you and I both understand about the diss is that it is not a diss to merely mention a name as a vehicle to end a line.

It is, however, a diss to name names as a vehicle for your own boasting, or to place someone in opposition to your own greatness. You know your way around the punch line better than anyone. Some might say you've mastered it—all of its darkness and light, all of the harsh angles that become soft enough to laugh off so rigorously that someone doesn't even realize the wound that has opened across their chest.

I loved you on "Jazz (We've Got)," even though I knew that when you spit out "strictly hardcore tracks, not a new jack swing," someone would have to pay for the offense. And who knew it would be Wreckx-N-Effect who would run into Q-Tip outside of a Run-DMC concert and punch him in the face, mad at your slight poke of fun at them? I guess the thing about being a fighter is that, sometimes, you start the fights you can't finish, and that's a part of brotherhood I know well even though I don't understand it myself. I have let my mouth write checks that my brothers, blood and not, have had to cash on my behalf, sometimes when I wasn't even around. If there is one thing to take from all of this talk of bassists throwing fists in bars and shooting guards with hot heads, it's that there's always something pulling them back to the calm and somewhat neutral middle. Starks had Ewing, yes. Jaco had the dual singing horns of the Weather Report to calm him.

You had Q-Tip, who would stand in front of a closed fist on the back of some slick shit you said to get a punch line off on a song about jazz and who did or did not have the jazz. I think there is a moment in here—when the fist left its mark on an eye in the name of anger—when Tribe truly became Tribe. When it was established that you all were brothers, willing to stand on one another. I love you on *The Low End Theory* for this and this alone: how unwilling you were to provoke in the name of something that might make a listener laugh for a while, and damn, did we need to laugh, because the police beat a man right there in the street and we all watched it on television, Phife. They didn't serve the time for it, either. So we all needed something foolish—a winding story about lost loves or a punch line about some wack shit. It's all low, all the time. Even the laughter is low. Even the way one exhales after a good laugh rumbles the walls of a room can sound like bass flooding out of the speakers.

CHAPTER FIVE

Award Tour

So many artists fail because they try to get it all back in one swing, or they remain stubborn, in the hope that the trends will switch back. Q-Tip and Ali Shaheed Muhammad had conquered the idea of jazz bleeding into hip-hop, but by 1993 the sound was changing, and they had the tools to change with it without the entire upheaval of their sound. *Midnight Marauders* was subtle in how it chose to catch up with the times. If hip-hop was to have a second wave, it needed A Tribe Called Quest with their ears to the West, unafraid and unthreatened.

Several things worked in favor of the West Coast in the early 1990s. Ice Cube had left N.W.A. in the late moments of 1989 over royalty disputes, leaving them without their chief songwriter and most versatile MC. In search of a solo career, Cube traveled east. He wanted to collaborate with chief N.W.A.

producer, Dr. Dre, on his first solo album but was not allowed to do so by Ruthless Records, who still held the rights to the N.W.A. members. When Cube approached Dre about working together, Ruthless Records boss Jerry Heller nixed the idea, telling Cube that Dre contractually couldn't work with any artists outside of N.W.A. This left Cube without a producer, and the West Coast had yet to develop a signature sound outside of what Dre was producing for the group. This left Cube as a bit of a man without a country. He was one of the first impactful West Coast MCs and writers, poised for a massive solo career, but he found himself handcuffed before getting it under way.

He linked with Dr. Dre's cousin, producer Sir Jinx, and they worked together to bring new life to piles of prewritten notebooks of lyrics that Cube had originally saved for Eazy-E before he decided to part with N.W.A. Like everyone else in rap, Cube had been tuned in to the sounds coming out of New York, just like rappers in New York were tuned in to N.W.A.— Tribe themselves used *Straight Outta Compton* as a template for the righteous anger resting underneath *The Low End Theory*. Cube, though, was more interested in the sounds being used by Public Enemy, who, by 1991, were four albums into their run as a fiercely political rap group that didn't sacrifice lyrics or beats to get their message across. To some, they were coastal siblings to N.W.A.—a group that was both unafraid and skilled at archiving their experience. Both groups were angry at the same system, but listening to *Straight Outta Compton* and *Fear of a Black Planet* back-to-back indicates something simple: the system has many hands and can place those hands around many necks at once.

More than just Public Enemy's lyrics and the siren-like bombast of Chuck D's voice, Ice Cube was drawn to the group because of their production. Public Enemy used an in-house production team known as the Bomb Squad, a group consisting of brothers Hank and Keith Shocklee, Eric "Vietnam" Sadler, Gary G-Wiz, and Bill Stephney.

What made the Bomb Squad perfect for Public Enemy and then Ice Cube was simple: they were unafraid to run directly into harsh, jarring sounds. If Phil Spector's wall of sound was based on the perfect placement of sound waves and instruments, speaking in harmony with one another, the Bomb Squad took that concept and turned it on its ear. Their motive was chaos, and they fought to arrive at that sonic chaos any way possible. Horns, sirens, bells, the sound of machinery clanking together: their sound was deep and dense, almost overwhelming. One might finish listening to a Public Enemy record on headphones and feel as if you just exited the gym, gasping and covered in sweat.

The Bomb Squad was using methods not at all unlike the methods Q-Tip was using at the same time with A Tribe Called Quest. Both were using samples as their primary weapons; it's just that Q-Tip was using the sample as a razor, and the Bomb Squad was using samples as a machine gun. What Q-Tip's ethos was—trimming the useful edges of a sample and blending multiple elements in the same song to create a type of harmony—was almost antithetical to what the Bomb Squad aimed for. While Q-Tip looked for connective tissue to create a single sound, the Bomb Squad was invested in piling noise on top of noise to create discord instead of harmony. This worked well, in part, because each member would work on their own aspect of a production in their own way before merging it with the other parts. Loops of sound would rest on top of other loops of sound. Samples were at odds with one another, seemingly speeding off a cliff but then coming together at the right moment.

Every full song on *Fear of a Black Planet* has at least three samples. Some have well over ten, like "Pollywanacraka," which samples a total of seventeen songs, from George Clinton to Boogie Down Productions. Where Tribe leaned into the lifting of jazz sounds to create their landscape, the Bomb Squad wanted anything loud and unsettling. They pulled from funk and the loudest and most chaotic of soul: James Brown, or "Holy Ghost" by the Bar-Kays. When that failed, the Bomb Squad would sample older Public Enemy songs, such as "Bring the Noise" on "Who Stole the Soul?" and "Show 'Em Whatcha Got" on "Revolutionary Generation."

If the wall of sound was initially created to find a home for every instrument in an attempt to let any listener in, the Bomb Squad was building a chaos loud enough to keep the wrong people out.

To be most effective, the Bomb Squad needed to craft its sound around a very particular type of MC. Chuck D was an obvious choice for Public Enemy: his voice was loud enough to work in concert with the clashing of sounds, and his flow was sharp and even enough to let the music work around him. He wasn't trying to overpower it so much as he was trying to find a way to live within it. It takes a special MC to find a comfortable pocket amid the hectic rage swelling out of the production of the Bomb Squad. It needs an MC who is equal parts ferocious and generous, willing to bow a bit to production even if it means slightly muting some of the MC's better instincts. It would take an MC who perhaps was used to being in a group already. That's what the Bomb Squad's beats were beckoning toward anyway—the music itself was a group inside a group. The band acted independently of whatever whims its leader might have. It was a question of control and who was willing to give themselves over to it.

Ice Cube wanted to echo that sound on 1990's *AmeriKKKa's Most Wanted*, his first album outside of N.W.A. He carried a bag overflowing with rhyme-filled notebooks and laid them at Hank Shocklee's feet. Recording began in the fall of 1989 and wrapped right before the album's release, in the early spring of 1990. Ice Cube is both Chuck D and not. His voice isn't the instrument that Chuck D's is, though the two are both deft dissectors of empire and systems. Cube not being as vocally bombastic as Chuck D didn't harm the work on *AmeriKKKa's Most Wanted*, as he's just as good—if not better—at finding pockets in his flow. True to their work with Public Enemy, the Bomb Squad made their production work on *AmeriKKKa's Most Wanted* a buffet of clashing samples, pulling fearlessly from multiple artists' back catalogs. "The Nigga Ya Love to Hate" sampled N.W.A.'s "Gangsta Gangsta"; "Turn Off the Radio" featured a sample from "Straight Outta Compton"; "Endangered Species (Tales from the Darkside)" sampled "Fuck Tha Police." The album's title track, which contains a total of fourteen samples—from Sly and the Family Stone to Richard Pryor—samples both "Fuck Tha Police" *and* "Straight Outta

Compton." Tongue-in-cheek as it might have been, it created an album as urgent and claustrophobic as it was meant to feel. It was an album that took the shape of an artist who left rap's most infamous group and was going to have to fight his way out of whatever came next.

The album was a critical and commercial success, going gold two weeks after it was released. Due to Cube's focusing his lens primarily on the narratives of south-central Los Angeles, the album was hailed as one of the West Coast's first master-pieces. The West Coast now had a solo MC respected by peers on the other coast, one that might challenge their supremacy. It didn't matter that *AmeriKKKa's Most Wanted* was recorded with East Coast producers at a studio in New York City. The West Coast was starting to plant its flag in the ground.

The complete dissolution of N.W.A. took place in 1991, when allegations arose that Eazy-E had signed over the group's contracts to Ruthless Records while holding on to a portion of N.W.A.'s publishing rights behind the group's back. The N.W.A. fallout—starting with Ice Cube's departure—began a series of events that would define the West Coast hip-hop moment of the early 1990s. After Ice Cube, the next biggest commodity in N.W.A. was Dr. Dre, the architect of the group's sound, who was seen as the kind of producer one could build an entire label around. Dre had become frustrated with what he saw as a lack of proper payment for the amount of work he was having to do under Ruthless Records, producing for nearly every artist under the label's imprint. He was a meticulous producer, one who was skilled enough to bow to the artists he was working with, as opposed to making artists follow his sound to his own creative ends. Like his peers on the East Coast, Dre did use samples, though he used significantly fewer than, say, Q-Tip and the Bomb Squad. Dre would, instead, have live musicians come in and closely re-create the sounds wanted on albums. It was a type of live sampling, heavy on synth notes and bass keyboards and flutes and saxophones. When N.W.A. fell apart for good, the genius of Dr. Dre was ripe for a new home—to the highest bidder.

This is where Suge Knight enters. He was a former football star who hailed from Compton, California. He'd gotten his start in the music industry working as a concert promoter and bodyguard for musicians after an NFL career didn't pan out. He began a music publishing company in 1989, which made its big break when Vanilla Ice agreed to sign over royalties from his hit "Ice Ice Baby" when it was found that the song contained material that was written by Suge Knight's client Mario Johnson. To help persuade Vanilla Ice, Knight allegedly entered his hotel room one night and threatened to dangle him by his ankles off a balcony. Knight became an effective businessman, but initially, he was in the business of fear. Fear as a currency can gain one actual currency, depending on how one uses the fear as a tactic to compel others.

In 1990, Knight went on to form an artist management company, signing already blooming West Coast artists DJ Quik and The D.O.C., both of whom introduced him to N.W.A. at a time when the group was in the midst of turmoil. In early 1991, Suge Knight teamed with The D.O.C. and SOLAR

Records founder Dick Griffey to start a record label that was first known as Future Shock Entertainment, and then known as Def Row, before ultimately settling on Death Row Records. When the label was established, Knight and his team anticipated the inevitable N.W.A. fallout, waiting for Dr. Dre to come to them. When they grew impatient with waiting—and when Jerry Heller insisted he was refusing to release Dr. Dre from his contract—Suge Knight and his cohorts approached Heller and Eazy-E with lead pipes and baseball bats, demanding the final release of Dr. Dre, The D.O.C., and Michel'le from their contracts. Fear, again, was worth more than money.

With that, Death Row Records was formed, a project that Knight insisted would evolve into the Motown of the nineties, with Dr. Dre as all parts Holland-Dozier-Holland, the songwriting trio associated with Motown. The success of Death Row relied entirely on Dr. Dre's first release, 1992's *The Chronic*. Some were skeptical, in part because Dre was never known as much of an MC, but this was quickly solved when Dr. Dre got his hands on a mixtape that featured a rapper with a smooth, lazy flow rhyming over the instrumental for En Vogue's "Hold On." Dre sought out Snoop Doggy Dogg and invited him to an audition, telling him that he was looking for rappers to fill out an album he was working on for a new label. Snoop aced the audition and pushed Dre to check out his old starting group, Tha Dogg Pound, consisting of rapper Kurupt and rapper/producer Daz Dillinger. The production group L.A. Posse sent Dr. Dre some of the tracks they had been working on in late 1991, and on the song "Niggas Come in All Colors," Dre was enamored with the lyrics and delivery of a woman MC, and he sought her out immediately. Lady of Rage was added to the team that was slowly building toward *The Chronic*. It was rounded out by rapper RBX and singer Nate Dogg, a cousin of Snoop.

With a roster strong enough to buoy an album's worth of Dre's production, which, by that point, had veered into chunky funk basslines and live, winding, screaming synths, Death Row Records seemed primed to soar. The production was groundbreaking for how much live instrumentation was forced into the studio, but also for sounding like the geography it was echoing.

When *The Chronic* was released, I listened to it as a child in a schoolyard park in the Midwest; it was winter, and I could feel the cold wind pushing into my coat, but for a moment, when the howling synth in "Let Me Ride" came on, I thought the sun had broken through and the cold briefly melted away. The sound was retrofitted, but it painted a landscape. New York production to that point worked from two ends of a spectrum: gritty and harsh or smoothed and sanitized. Dr. Dre's G-funk operated somewhere in the middle. He was trying to create a visual space for the music to live beyond the record. Through the speakers, one could see cars with their tops dropped, sand from a beach filling up the hardwood floors of a too-small apartment, blue and red bandannas around every corner of a wall.

The Chronic, at its best, is both album and picture book. I knew very little of 1960s Impalas or Dayton Rims. In the Midwest, people didn't equip their cars the way cars were equipped on the West Coast, largely because of the instability of the weather. But, even before setting eyes on the music videos associated with the album, I could listen to the music, close my eyes, and visualize the cars rolling in straight lines down sun-soaked roads with palm trees hanging over them lazily, letting their wide leaves cast shadows. I loved *The Chronic* for the windows into the world it opened for me, but it served a greater purpose. If Ice Cube gave the West Coast a viable solo MC, *The Chronic* gave the West Coast a viable sound and a label to house that sound. Death Row Records had their first major success with *The Chronic*'s release. The album spent eight months on the Billboard 200 chart, with its three singles becoming Top 10 hits as well. It eventually went triple platinum. But beyond its sales, *The Chronic* introduced a new stable of West Coast artists, steeped in versatility, that shifted hip-hop's focus away from its birthplace.

By 1993, A Tribe Called Quest had largely avoided any significant drama, outside of Q-Tip's minor scuffle with Wreckx-N-Effect. True to their previous practice, they began the year working on what was next. Having not only survived the test of the sophomore album but passed it with flying colors, A Tribe Called Quest was now a known commodity, with a sound being hailed as the future of the genre. Where the work of Q-Tip on the first two albums was to build a sound and then turn it on its ear, the work of this next album was to bridge the gaps between those two elements—to settle on a sound that would carry the group through what seemed as if it would be a long and deep career.

What wasn't going to be sacrificed was the bass-heavy sound that flooded *The Low End Theory*. That concept remained, along with the renewed idea that Tribe was now a group with two distinctly different MCs who complemented each other well enough for the group to have a discussion about making music with the voice as an instrument—reflecting how Q-Tip and Phife could each bend similar sounds to their liking. To get to work on the album, Q-Tip eschewed the traditional studio approach and set up his production equipment in the basement of Phife's grandmother's house. She gave him a key so he could come and go as he pleased, leading Q-Tip to map out late-night planning sessions for the album. It created a more casual atmosphere, one that better suited Phife's creative process, as he could sit and watch basketball or play video games while listening to the beats Q-Tip was cooking up, lazily flowing over them when things organically came to him. The rigor of their first two projects bore significant fruit, but they were hard on Phife, who was consistently exhausted due to his diabetes and the energy it required of him to tour and write and perform interviews. His exhaustion led naturally to Q-Tip shouldering most of the group's publicity appearances. But behind the scenes, Q-Tip was also working to make the production and recording space more comfortable. Though the motive was not explicit, there was a perceived generosity in the shift of recording style and session from the past two albums to the album that would become *Midnight Marauders*. Phife could be in a safe and comfortable place, where he would be at his sharpest. This served the group, as well—Phife was at his best when he was relaxed and playful, when the pressure to rise to Q-Tip's level wasn't explicit and present.

By the time these recording sessions were going on, Q-Tip was also sought after as an in-demand producer independent of the group. Nas, then an up-and-coming solo MC who was seen as the next evolution of Rakim, asked Q-Tip to produce his single "One Love," which was on the solo album, *Illmatic*, he was preparing for a 1994 release. Q-Tip had also worked on Run-DMC's *Down with the King* album and a track for another up-and-coming MC from New Jersey, Apache. While this didn't impact his work for his own group, it did broaden his sense of sounds and what he was capable of. Producing for a wider range of MCs with different skill sets allowed him to return to the *Midnight Marauders* sessions renewed, with a new set of sounds to play with. His skills on the production side moved past his singular ability to stack loops and evolved into extracting subtle sounds from sample sources and stitching them together cleanly. There is a more controlled restraint in the production of *Marauders*, like the subtle sample on "Award Tour" of just the keys on Milt Jackson's "Olinga," which is used to flesh out the song's other elements but not dragged to the forefront, as Tip might have done on Tribe's earlier albums. He was understanding how to make the sound bend to his ideas without forcing its movement.

Midnight Marauders was to be the Tribe Called Quest album that they entered into as a known commodity and most comfortable with one another. They faced pressure from the outside—the question of "Can they do it again?" loomed heavy in the industry. *People's Instinctive Travels* gained the group a surprising notoriety among the underground rap elite, and *The Low End Theory* was a bona fide success, which primed the group for what some thought would be an inevitable letdown. Jarobi White, who left the group again halfway through the recording of *The Low End Theory*, was welcomed back into recording sessions, but merely as comic relief. When pressure in the sessions got too high, he would come in the studio and make jokes or do impressions until everyone in the studio was doubled over in laughter. Tribe had to stay loose during the making of the album. When the stakes are high, the hardest thing to do is not succumb to the stress that accompanies them.

In some ways, *Midnight Marauders* is the great Tribe album. It might not be the most perfect Tribe album—though it is yet another classic—but it is the album on which Q-Tip and Phife were most tuned in to each other's needs and desires. With regard to the production, Q-Tip and Ali Shaheed Muhammad worked to maintain an eclectic sample base, but—perhaps responding to the shift in sound coming from the West—Q-Tip substituted funk samples for jazz ones, giving the album a denser sound, which was complemented by the layering of drums.

Years later, in 2012, Tip would elaborate on this, saying that when he went into the studio for everything after *The Low End Theory*, he thought of himself as competing with Dr. Dre. "Everybody deals with shit in a competitive way. But not in like an egregious way, how shit looks a little bit today," he explained in a radio interview on Shade 45's *All Out Show*. "But more like one-upsmanship in the music. Tryin' to stay fresh

. . . just keeping your eye on that dude. And for me, person-ally, when I went in, that dude was Dre. The bar was set very high. Musically, my main thing was Dre. That was like trying to make something he would like and appreciate in a way. Musically. The group was N.W.A., and to me, that was the benchmark." In this way, the work was an exchange, similar to the 1960s, when Brian Wilson was pushed by and pushing the Beatles. Although the coasts were drifting apart in some ways, Q-Tip was driven enough by the sounds coming out of the West to try and hold the region close.

Now it was the Meters, the Ohio Players, and James Brown when once it was Eric Dolphy. The album also used fewer sam-ples than their previous work, with most songs having only two or three, instead of the sprawling number on their earlier releases. The album's samples, like the Bomb Squad's, also began to nod back to the hip-hop before it. On "We Can Get Down," Ali Shaheed Muhammad dices up Eric B. and Rakim's "My Melody," and "The Chase" borrows elements from Biz Markie's "Nobody Beats the Biz."

The album is diverse in sound and topic, with Q-Tip—the group's deft romantic—making a canvas of the sexy and well-paced "Electric Relaxation," and Phife going on lyri-cal runs that don't allow a listener to get up off the mat. On "Award Tour":

> I have a quest to have a mic in my hand
> Without that, it's like Kryptonite and Superman
> So Shaheed come in with the sugar cuts
> Phife Dawg's my name, but on stage, call me Dynomutt

When was the last time you heard the Phifer sloppy
Lyrics anonymous, you'll never hear me copy

On "Oh My God," he's his classic balance of deprecating and triumphant:

Some brothers try to diss but Malik, you see 'em bitching
Me no care about them dibby MC, my shit is hitting
Trini gladiator, anti-hesitater
Shaheed push the fader from here to Grenada
Mr Energetic, who me sound pathetic?
When's the last time you heard a funky diabetic?

Throughout, Tip and Phife are no longer pushing each other toward some imagined greater heights, but the rappers have seen the goal; they know exactly how high it is, and they spend an entire album boosting each other toward it. Tip, cupping his hands for his brother to place a foot into, and Phife doing the same.

It is important to talk about the album's cover now. A Tribe Called Quest were not often fixtures on their album covers anyway, so the fact that their faces don't show up on the cover of *Midnight Marauders* isn't much of a surprise. But it's who was on the cover that makes it interesting, given the time when it was released.

Q-Tip didn't want to part with the idea of the red, black, and green–striped woman who had adorned the previous album's cover. He wanted her on a bed at first, wearing headphones with her hand on her crotch. The label rejected that. He then wanted to have her walking in front of the Flatiron Building in New York with headphone jacks coming out of her head, with connected headphones being worn by a group of people following behind her. The photo shoot for this failed, and the idea was nixed.

In the end, the two concepts blended, somewhat. On the *Midnight Marauders* cover as it stands, the striped woman appears, legs spread and hands joined downward, near her crotch. Wearing headphones behind her is a mass of familiar faces. To get the cover right, A Tribe Called Quest reached out to various hip-hop artists they respected from everywhere hip-hop was currently being made and asked if they could get a headshot with them wearing headphones. The artists were all supposed to put on headphones and make a face as though they were listening to the album for the first time. What began as a small idea bloomed into a significantly greater one. By the time the project was complete, the album was overflowing with faces of collaborators, peers, and respected icons of the industry: Chuck D, Grandmaster Flash, Daddy-O of Stetsasonic, Oakland rapper Too Short, Beastie Boys MCA and Mike D, Ice-T, Pee Wee Dance from the Rock Steady Crew, Ant Banks, Special K of the Awesome Two, Chi-Ali, all the members of the Bay-area rap group The Pharcyde, A-Plus from Souls of Mischief, Buckshot from Black Moon, and a handful of other rap luminaries, both new and emerging, including Dr. Dre, and a little-known record man named Sean "Puffy" Combs.

It was a small show of unity, which echoed large as hip-hop's coasts began to fracture more loudly. Something was brewing on the horizon, though Tribe didn't know that at the time. It's a pure nod to what they loved about hip-hop, and the people they loved who were making it. The *Midnight Marauders* album cover is a who's who of the genre in its 1993 state. I would sit with the small cassette tape in my room, unraveling it and seeing how many faces I could point out without looking at the names on the back—seeing who might be hidden among the background, headphones on, mouth agape with wonder.

This gesture—though it may have seemed small at the time—acted as a point of pride for Tribe and was something deeply in line with their ethos. They were proud New Yorkers, of course. But they were chasing good sound, and would consume it wherever it arose. A Tribe Called Quest listened to N.W.A. to make *The Low End Theory*, at a time when Ice Cube ventured east to make his first solo masterpiece, and shortly after that, A Tribe Called Quest turned back to what was bubbling out of the West to inform their newer, harder sound. The *Midnight Marauders* cover is a nod to who and what had managed to carry A Tribe Called Quest to that point. At a time when the two coasts were engaged in harmless but escalating sniping, A Tribe Called Quest was giving thanks, endlessly.

This album was a quicker success than the first two, registering a gold certification with sales of 500,000 only about two months after its release. Its songs were played on radio, particularly "Award Tour," the first Tribe song I remember memorizing from front to back. It seemed, in the moment, that A Tribe Called Quest was immovable.

There was another reason why *Midnight Marauders* contained fewer samples than the albums before it. The golden age of sampling in hip-hop took place from about 1987 to 1992. In this time, record companies still seemed to think that hip-hop was going to come and go, so they didn't pay much attention to what the artists in the genre were doing or how they were using their music. This gave artists the ability to do what Tribe and Public Enemy were doing—layering massive amounts of samples one on top of the other. Lawyers didn't care, labels didn't care, and it was virtually a free-for-all.

In late 1991, Grand Upright Music sued Warner Brothers because Gilbert O'Sullivan's song publisher noticed that Biz Markie's song "Alone Again" made a clear and obvious use of O'Sullivan's original song of the same title. It seemed obvious to O'Sullivan that this shouldn't be allowed without some legal recourse. The song belonged to O'Sullivan, after all, and he was getting no financial gain from it. Sampling is creativity until a judge decides it is theft, and that is what a judge did— going so far as to suggest that Biz Markie should serve jail time for his appropriation of the song. Right after that, the Turtles brought a suit against De La Soul for using elements from "You Showed Me."

Those two lawsuits opened up the floodgates and instilled fear into record companies, who realized that their back catalogs were all getting sampled freely, sometimes by artists they had signed to their label. The industry acted quickly before more lawsuits came down, setting a rule that if you release a record on any major label, you have to clear a sample.

"Clearing a sample" means that a fee has to be paid to whatever entity holds the rights to the sample, that is, whoever owns the actual sound recording, and whoever the song publisher is. So, one is paying for both the sound and the melody underneath the sound. The process takes a lot of money and time—labels weren't willing to spend the former, and artists weren't willing to spend the latter. And even if both were willing to, there was no guarantee that the rights-holders would allow the sample to be cleared. And if one was, but the other wasn't, the sample couldn't be used. Albums from the early 1990s that were built atop a mountain of samples became impossible and too time-consuming to make. The average price to clear a single sample could reach tens of thousands of dollars, which made albums with over ten samples per song just not financially viable anymore, particularly when some labels were still not sold on rap's longevity and were concerned about sinking so much money into it. Dr. Dre found a way around this on *The Chronic* by re-creating the sounds of old songs with live musicians, manipulating notes here and there to lessen the number of samples he used. He was also fortunate to latch on to George Clinton, who was more than willing to hand over much of the Parliament-Funkadelic catalog for a fraction of the cost that others were charging. Dre built a sound on what was affordable, but some of his peers weren't so fortunate and didn't have the resources he had.

This was how the sun began to go down on rap's golden era of sound. Sampling provided more than just a backbone for the music; it was a way to get a new generation to engage with the history of sounds the new music was pulling from.

A lot of the music being sampled was rooted in past political moments, finding its way to newer political narratives by being pulled tight over a track where MCs would rap about their own desires for a fractured world. Sampling created a dialogue between past and present and helped bridge a gap between the music a rapper was first introduced to and the music they desperately wanted to share with the new world.

When the smoke cleared, everything felt like it required more work. Production styles had to adjust. Single or fewer samples had to be stretched out over fuller portions of a song. Fewer gems could be found hiding beneath tracks, waiting to be unearthed by a close listener. Producers like Pete Rock and the Bomb Squad suffered, and they saw their output first slightly decline and then drastically decline. The time it took to make albums grew, so the space needed between releases grew, thus the anticipation revolving around releases grew, and so disappointment was often plentiful. A Tribe Called Quest released one of the last great albums of rap's first golden era, and they had to find out how to survive whatever was coming next.

CHAPTER SIX

1nce Again

There is a cost to moving the world—a cost that one perhaps doesn't consider when pushing an entire sound or genre or country forward. With your hands on the machinery of whatever you imagine progress to be, it is difficult to imagine the real-time drawbacks. Especially if you are immersed in it. The problem that A Tribe Called Quest found themselves wrestling with in 1996 was the perfect storm of several things. First, rap's landscape had very literally shifted. *Midnight Marauders* was released in November of 1993, on the same day as another hotly anticipated rap album: a debut from the Staten Island rap group Wu-Tang Clan.

Wu-Tang Clan's structure was mostly unique to the rap landscape of the 1990s because of its sheer size. At the time of the album's release, the group had nine MCs and an MC/

producer in Rza. What made the engines turn on Wu-Tang Clan was specifically the fact that there was no drop-off in skill from each of the MCs. On the album, it was hard to find any weak link in the group, as if they were each born to play their deeply specific role in the makeup of the band. Even Ol' Dirty Bastard, first introduced to the world on the first verse and chorus of the iconic song "Shame on a Nigga," was a vital cog in the machine—a less structured MC and more a hybrid of Flavor Flav and Eazy-E, he added a levity to the group's grimy exterior. To pick a favorite rapper out of the group's lineup on the first album was impossible. For a moment, it would seem that the star was Method Man, the tall and charismatic MC with an uneven but inviting flow. And then, before that thought could settle, it would seem that it might be Raekwon or Ghostface Killah, both storytellers with inviting but deeply unreliable narration, which added to the album's tone and intrigue. The star might be Rza, the producer who crafted the sound that turned out to be the blueprint for the future of what some would call hardcore hip-hop.

And that was it, too: the sound. What Rza was able to do was a sharp departure from what was happening before. The goal of the album *Enter the Wu-Tang (36 Chambers)*, sonically, was to find a way to shift the gritty underground sounds into something that was digestible for the mainstream. In a way, this was catapulting off the success of a blueprint that A Tribe Called Quest had laid out, but Rza was interested in a sound that was darker. There were samples on the album, yes. But with the new sampling laws coming into effect right before the album's creation, the samples were fewer and further between. Additionally, the samples were voice-heavy, particularly thick with dialogue from martial arts films that were cult classics, like *Five Deadly Venoms* and *Shaolin and Wu Tang*. "Da Mystery of Chessboxin'" starts with a combination of dialogue from both films that weaves together seamlessly:

> *A game of chess is like a swordfight:*
> *You must think first before you move*
> *Toad style is immensely strong*
> *And immune to nearly any weapon*
> *When it's properly used it's almost invincible.*

The first two lines are from *Shaolin and Wu-Tang*, and the last three are from *Five Deadly Venoms*. They weave together so well in both sound and topic that it's hard to imagine them as disparate. This trick is pulled a handful of times on the album, blending dialogue from separate films and pushing them together within the context of a single song. What Rza may have been getting at here, then, is the idea of pulling at the edges of anything that might fit together, and throwing it all in the same pot until everything found its own harmony. That is the ethos of the Wu-Tang Clan. Many of the MCs spent the nineties (and beyond) cultivating flourishing solo careers, but on the albums with the group, each still managed to flourish, and to do so without sacrificing much of their skill set. It was something that most other rap groups hadn't figured out yet, even the successful ones. There's a way to look at this that says there were no weak links in the Clan, but there's another way that says any weakness that any member had was eliminated

by the ways each member of the group could so richly prior-
itize their strengths. It's something Tribe hadn't figured out
until about an album and a half in, despite their success.

Rza's dialogue-based samples paired with heavy and
haunting string melodies or sharp and jarring organs. When
there were samples of jazz and soul, they were often perfunc-
tory—exercises to build a small part of the canvas that Rza was
later coloring over with paint of his own making. There were
exceptions to this—the soaring Gladys Knight and the Pips
sample on "Can It Be All So Simple" howls through the song
like a renegade wind. But largely, the samples aren't the stars
of the show, rather the manipulation of the samples is. Rza
gets the samples to bend until they are hardly noticeable, and
I imagine this, too, is a type of hard core—to put hands around
the neck of a sound until it is reborn as a new sound.

It also created a reliance on soul music samples that was,
at the time, less heard of. A loophole that Rza found was that
soul samples were slightly easier to clear and a bit less expen-
sive than the jazz and old rock samples that some of his peers
had relied on. And if he viewed the main function of the sample as something to be manipulated, it almost didn't matter
what it's original form was. Of course, about a decade later,
rap music would live through an entire era dedicated almost
entirely to the manipulation of the soul sample. But in the
moment, it was a novel concept, especially that of washing
over the sample with such richly violent instrumentation.
This style of production opened doors for producers like
Havoc, who shaped the sound of Mobb Deep's early albums
from Rza's blueprint, most noticeably on the 1996 album

Hell on Earth, which is sparse and beautiful, and would per-haps sound best playing over a graveyard on a cloud-filled day while tree branches trembled under the weight of a hundred black birds.

Mobb Deep was in many ways a group very much like Tribe themselves. Like Tribe, they were from Queens. Like Tribe, their music relied on a producer who took on rapping duties and a rapper who worked in harmony with the producer as best he could. Like the members of Tribe, Havoc and Prodigy were childhood friends who aspired to be rappers, and chased after the dream until they made it happen. Like Tribe, Mobb Deep released their first album—1993's *Juvenile Hell*—when they were just teens, and though it had some marginal suc-cess, they didn't gain their footing until they figured out their formula on their second album, the critically and commer-cially successful *The Infamous*, released in 1995. The difference between the two groups was perhaps not in the way they saw the world, but in the way they manifested their seeing of the world. Mobb Deep was rugged and cynical. The Queens they wrote about was one that was a place merely to survive at all costs. Their music was laced with a type of fear and paranoia that bled through the sonic landscape: an avalanche of drums from each direction; a sharp synth slicing through like a knife; piano loops and distorted bass lines that sounded like they could have been pulled out of a horror film.

Havoc didn't know much of anything about production when he decided to take on the majority of production duties for *The Infamous*; he just knew that the group couldn't afford to keep sifting through producers to find things they would often discard. "We started producing because other producers was giving us shit that we didn't like, or they was just charging too much," Havoc said in Brian Coleman's *Check the Technique: Liner Notes for Hip-Hop Junkies.* So he figured he could do it himself.

A little-known fact about *The Infamous* is that when the group was trying to find their way in the studio in the early months of 1994, a fan of their music reached out. Q-Tip had heard a song called "Shook Ones" that was starting to circulate in the underground rap circles in New York. Intrigued, and fascinated by the idea of a Queensbridge collaboration—and currently in between projects himself—he dropped in on the group in the studio. By then a somewhat sought-after studio mind, Q-Tip was in awe of how the group had taken to crafting their own sound. The engineer that was assigned to work on the album wasn't interested, largely because of the group's reputation for how they spent their studio time. Weed, guns, fights, and dice games would all spill out at any given time, so the label-picked engineer wasn't exactly as interested in being hands-on with the group. Q-Tip, however, was more than equipped to speak the group's language and act as a type of translator between the engineer and the group itself, before he took over much of the mixing duties himself.

Q-Tip hadn't really engineered as much as he'd produced, but he took to it well. Havoc's ability to layer music gently and to articulate what each song needed made Q-Tip's job easy. Havoc, a fan of Tribe, knew that Q-Tip could figure out drums in a way that he couldn't yet, so Q-Tip's main function was to move sounds around to best accent the other sounds. "Put your shit on it," Havoc would tell Q-Tip while playing him new records. Q-Tip, for his part, told Havoc that what would really bring out some of the hardcore elements they were reaching for in the album was if they leaned into the idea of using major chords on the album, and let the instruments really take up space and linger. You hear this on a song like "Survival of the Fittest," where a piano riff swells and swells, stepping heavily over the drums and horn. Q-Tip was invaluable to the album's process, mixing eight of the songs and coproducing the songs "Temperature's Rising," "Give Up the Goods," and "Drink Away the Pain" under the name "The Abstract."

On "Give Up the Goods," particularly, one can hear Q-Tip's touch—the way the high hats lend a smoothness over the otherwise heavy weight of the song. It provided a glimpse into how Tribe could find its way to maneuver this new direction of rap. It was the excitement that Q-Tip saw and heard in the exuberant ear of Havoc that perhaps sparked a renewed excitement. Mobb Deep was Tribe through a funhouse mirror of despair, righteous anger, violence, and the rich ability to articulate it all without any softening. Rap was starting to go to a place Tribe hadn't shown they could reach yet, and the stakes were high for the group all over again.

The cloud had not only descended lower but had also managed to spread. Between the years of 1993 and 1996, rap had become more entrenched not only in a coastal battle but in the blossoming of regional sounds. By 1996, Outkast had come along, debuting with *Southernplayalisticadillacmuzik* in 1994, and really cementing themselves as leaders of the new southern sound with *ATLiens* in 1996, with its space-funk and reverb, creating an atmosphere that felt both futuristic and also distinctly southern. Also out of Atlanta, Jermaine Dupri's So So Def record label was gaining its footing, releasing albums by Da Brat and Kris Kross to establish themselves. Beyond that, by 1996, Master P's No Limit Records was blooming out of New Orleans, with his *Ice Cream Man* album being a surprise success, followed by Silkk the Shocker's *The Shocker* as another hit. While this output was promising for the lifespan of the genre as a whole, it was one small part of a larger storm brewing along the coasts, both of which had felt largely alone in their territories and now had an escalation of talent and tension coming for them. Everything in the genre became louder by default.

It is hard to say exactly when the boiling point occurred. I like to think that there were several boiling points, and they simply kept speeding past one another, until the temperature was simply no longer manageable for anyone. But if there is a prominent boiling point to turn to, it can be said that the 1995 Source Awards changed the trajectory of rap's tensions. By that point, Death Row Records was a viable and respected institution on the West Coast, and Puff Daddy's Bad Boy Records, led by the breakout star the Notorious B.I.G., was climbing the ladder on the East Coast. Puff Daddy was the label head and main face of the brand. He was charismatic and played a very particular role in the career of his artists, B.I.G. specifically. Puff began as an intern at Uptown Records, where he helped develop the career of Mary J. Blige and gained a reputation as both a keen eye for talent and someone who was more than equipped at not only starting a party but also keeping a party going. By 1993, during the recording of the Notorious B.I.G.'s debut album, *Ready to Die*, Puff's ego and vision began to confuse and frustrate his coworkers at Uptown, and label head Andre Harrell had seen enough. He couldn't manage both his label *and* the intern he hired at his label, so he let Puff go, and told him to take B.I.G. with him. From the ashes rose Bad Boy Records, and East Coast rap's newest star. Biggie was wildly skilled and also a character: he was a large, dark-skinned MC who was both deeply streetwise and also very invested in cultivating his image as a lover—someone who desired women and was equally desired by them. This formula made *Ready to Die* a runaway critical and commercial success. Biggie could rap, but he could also be sold to an audience with relative ease. What helped was that Puff Daddy was his hype man, a role he played in the visual aesthetics of all Bad Boy artists, but none as well as he did with Biggie. Puff was a hovering presence in every sound, every visual, as either an ad lib or a wave of ad libs, such as dancing in videos. He both wasn't and was an artist. Bad Boy's advantage was almost unfair in its earliest days. It had not only one of the greatest new artists in rap music but also an executive producer who had the style, charisma, and ego to eclipse most artists on every other label, without even rapping a verse. Puff Daddy knew what Suge Knight knew: the game, at some point, had to sell. And nothing sells like conflict.

The thing about the 1995 Source Awards is that they should have been a celebration of hip-hop's evolution. That was the second full-fledged year of the Source Awards, which started out as a kind of sideshow on *Yo! MTV Raps* in 1991. The 1995 Source Awards were a full-on production, staged at Madison Square Garden for the second year. In 1994, the awards came and went with very little tension but for one moment: during a performance mix-up, an energetic 2Pac took the stage with his entourage at the same time that Q-Tip was scheduled to take the stage and present an award. 2Pac's music began playing from a DAT tape, and he and his group ran out and started performing, while Q-Tip stood at the side of the stage, bewildered. It was a common awards show mix-up, with likely no ill intent behind it. But with the already rising tensions between the coasts, even in mid-1994, neither party could be sure. Members of 2Pac's group and members of Zulu Nation exchanged sharp words, but the altercation never escalated to physical violence.

Just months later, in November of 1994, 2Pac was shot five times while exiting a New York City recording studio. Shortly thereafter, he vocally insisted that his once friend but new rival the Notorious B.I.G. may have had something to do with the setup. And so, by the time the 1995 Source Awards rolled around, the East Coast–West Coast feud had imprinted its name on bullets that echoed through the skin of one of rap's brightest young stars. Rather than back down, both coasts responded with a harsher, more arrogant approach.

At the time of the awards, 2Pac was in jail, stemming from a sexual assault charge. Suge Knight had yet to bail him out and align him with Death Row Records, but that plan was brewing. Meanwhile, the East Coast backlash to the rising tide of the West Coast was at an all-time high. Death Row Records was thriving on the back of Dr. Dre and Snoop Dogg, who released his critically acclaimed debut album, *Doggystyle*, just a year earlier in 1993. On top of this, many in East Coast rap circles took offense to 2Pac pointing fingers at Bad Boy Records with what seemed like little proof. Bad Boy wasn't entirely beloved, but they were still worthy of being protected.

Suge Knight and Death Row Records personnel crossed the country for the Source Awards and ended up sitting to the left of the aisle in the front row. Puff Daddy and Bad Boy records staff were aligned on the other side of the aisle, in the front row to the right. Here is the thing you may remember: Suge Knight, massive and cloaked in red, grabbing the microphone with gold adorning his wrists, and declaring:

"Any artist out there that wanna be an artist, stay a star, and won't have to worry about the executive producer trying to be all in the videos, all on the records, dancing—come to Death Row!"

It was early in the show, an opening shot fired across the bow that echoed through the night. What happened throughout the rest of the show created the true architecture for version 2.0 of the East Coast–West Coast feud. Now that the guns had been drawn in the first act and fired in the third, no stakes were too high, no sentiment too bold to attach to one's name. During Bad Boy's performance at the awards, a charged-up Puff Daddy grabs the mic and yells: "I LIVE IN THE EAST, AND I'M GONNA DIE IN THE EAST!" much to the joy of the crowd. Later, when Snoop Dogg takes the stage, he is booed roundly, and somewhere at the intersection of pride and pain, he stands back:

"The East Coast ain't got no love for Snoop Dogg? The East Coast ain't got no love for Snoop Dogg and Death Row?"

The crowd continues booing, confirming that it does, in fact, not have love for Snoop Dogg and Death Row.

"All right, well let it be known, then," says Snoop, before storming off stage.

And then, up comes Outkast, merely collateral damage on the predetermined battlefield. When they won Best New Artist, the crowd began booing again. By this point in the night, there was almost a knee-jerk reaction to anything that wasn't New York. A young André 3000 accepted the award, scowling at the audience, and becoming prophetic.

"The South got something to say, that's all I got to say."

When the curtain went down on the Source Awards in 1995, hip-hop was fractured—into a land of many tribes, a country of many countries, seemingly drifting aggressively apart, with blood starting to faintly spread across the sky.

Beats, Rhymes and Life was released in the middle of the summer in 1996, which was a good time in one of rap's best years. There was enough sound variance to offset the coastal bitterness boiling underneath. The Fugees released *The Score* that winter, an eclectic and brilliant album that soared to the top of the charts. In the spring, Tribe's old Native Tongues mate Busta Rhymes released his debut album *The Coming*, featuring production by The Ummah—a collective composed of Q-Tip, Ali Shaheed Muhammad, and J Dilla—and a guest verse from Q-Tip. Busta's unparalleled style and energy took the rap world by storm, and the album was a hit, boosted by its single "Woo-Hah!! Got You All in Check," which was played up in a colorful video directed by Hype Williams, with Q-Tip and Phife appearing in cameos. Earlier in the summer, the anticipated debut solo album by Jay-Z, *Reasonable Doubt*, dropped, presenting a new direction for storytelling rap: the hustler made good, as if Al Pacino survived the bullets in *Scarface*. In July, right before Tribe's album was released, De La Soul released *Stakes Is High*, an album that was well received but furthered their departure from their early Native Tongues sound. It was their last album for four years. Nas—rap's golden child just two years earlier—also released his second album, *It Was Written*, the follow-up to his debut classic, *Illmatic*.

So by the time *Beats, Rhymes and Life* came into the world in late July, the table had already been set. Rap was having one of its most successful years since its inception, and radio was hungry for it. It can be argued that all Tribe had to do was not fall on their faces, and they didn't. It was the start of a decline, sure—maybe. But there are so few mountains higher than the mountain A Tribe Called Quest found themselves on after their first three albums, and the world around them was changing. It is better to stay largely where you are than attempt to go higher and have a whole world notice your falling.

It isn't like Tribe lay dormant from 1993 to 1996. At the peak of their powers after *Midnight Marauders*, and with enough notable and memorable material to support them, they toured extensively for nearly three years straight, taking little time off from the road. This upset the natural order of their production process. Their first few albums worked so well because they felt like one continuous piece of music: sessions for one album would end and spill over into sessions for a new album. Tribe was never not working on the next thing, until the next thing was all about how many shows they could pack into a week or a month or a year. They were both stagnant and not. It's hard to innovate the new when thousands of voices are still singing along to the old. They weren't able to turn corners as fast as they were before, when their entire mindset going into a project revolved around being able to rush into and play off of whatever new sounds hip-hop was offering. Because so much of their time was spent on the road, or with Q-Tip working on non-Tribe projects, the group was treading water for the first time in their careers.

On top of this, Phife moved to Atlanta after recording *Midnight Marauders*—in part because he thought the breakup of Tribe was an inevitability after that album. *Midnight Marauders* had been the group's most difficult album to make. Despite—or perhaps because of—the sacrifices made to comfort each member, infighting in the group escalated, until it got to a point where the group's tours were no longer sunny affairs, and their chemistry began to spiral in early 1994. Phife found himself exhausted by New York and the impact it was having on his health. He wanted to start a family, and Atlanta, at the time, was intriguing. A burgeoning rap hotbed like New York was in the late 1970s and early 1980s, Atlanta was slower paced and less demanding. Phife had in some ways decided that he was done with the group before the group was officially done.

On the other side, Q-Tip decided to convert to Islam in 1994.

He had previously been leaning toward Islam, but a reading of the Quran refueled his desire for faith, and he became devout. By the time A Tribe Called Quest set out to record their new album in 1995, the group's chemistry had entirely shifted. Phife would have to travel up from Atlanta to record, and sometimes the studio would be entirely empty when he arrived. Anticipating that Phife's input could potentially be minimal or inconsistent, Q-Tip added his cousin, a young rapper named Consequence, to flesh out the group's rapping and fill in some verses in spots. Additionally, in 1996, the production team expanded to become The Ummah, Arabic for "Community."

This is when the legend of J Dilla begins. In 1995, during the making of the *Beats, Rhymes and Life* album, Dilla was a twenty-one-year-old phenom from Detroit, who had little experience producing except for some underground work in his hometown. Less than a year later, he would have formed Slum Village and begun to cement his sound, but in 1995, he was a producer Ali and Tip had an eye on, thinking that he might help transition their group's sound.

Dilla's reputation had preceded him, even with his minimal output in 1995. His parents claim that Dilla could match pitch-perfect harmony by the age of two months, and that he began collecting vinyl before he could read. As a child, he spun records in Detroit parks for recreation. Much like Q-Tip, he took up beat making in high school using tape decks as his studio. He trained himself on stop tapes, drawing sample sounds from his massive record collection.

In this way, Dilla was a perfect fit to fold in with the desired evolution of Tribe. He was of the same generation as Q-Tip, with a similar self-taught technique but a different sound palette and execution. Dilla was utilizing unique and unexpected drum sounds and unconventional sample chops that dipped heavily into 1960s rock and soul.

All of this meant that Dilla was supposed to push Tribe toward a more modern sound. Gone on *Beats, Rhymes and Life* was their characteristic bottom-heavy, thick bass, replaced by a newer, airy and soul-sample-based quality, rooted in tricks that would become Dilla's signature. This album's sample template was significantly smaller, with most songs having only one sample and a few having none at all. The album essentially showcased J Dilla's blooming talents. It took Dilla mere minutes to make some beats on the record, like the ominous and sparse "Get a Hold," the second song on the album, which features samples from William DeVaughn's "Be Thankful for What You Got" and The Cyrkle's "The Visit." According to Shoes, a collaborator of Dilla's, it took him twelve minutes total—most of the time was spent getting the drums. Once he got those, he chopped the sample and put the loop on top in three minutes. Where Tip was meticulous and microscopic in his pursuit of perfection, Dilla was immediate and haphazardly brilliant, and he provided the group with a sonic balance.

The world already knew what Q-Tip could do and, on a slightly lesser scale, what Ali Shaheed Muhammad could do. Dilla was a talented but unknown entity. *Beats, Rhymes and Life* gave the group an opportunity to see if they could catch on to rap's newer production waves, but it also gave Q-Tip an opportunity to scale back the burden of carrying the group's sound.

The creation process with the album felt, at times, as if there were two entirely different groups working on the project. Newly converted to Islam, Q-Tip and Ali Shaheed Muhammad would take breaks during the album's creation to make prayer, which made Phife uncomfortable and widened the distance between members of the group.

The album's first single was "1nce Again," which featured R&B singer Tammy Lucas and sampled Cannonball Adderley's "Untitled" and Gary Burton's "I'm Your Pal." That they lead with a single that sampled two jazz acts is the first part of the lie: Tribe wanting their audience to think that they're actually who they've always been, returned after three years to the same clothes they left in the closet, and they all still fit fine.

The single opens with a familiar refrain:

"You on point, Phife?"

"Once again, Tip."

It is a callback to five years prior, on *The Low End Theory*'s "Check the Rhime," where Q-Tip poses the same question, and Phife responds with "All the time, Tip." This, perhaps, is the second part of the lie, or the part that exposes the lie more clearly: a group known for pushing boundaries, relying on their own nostalgia in an era that no longer felt like their era. Rap was no longer as sample based, and when it returned to being sample-heavy just a few years later, the approach to sampling would have changed. The divide between that which was commercial and that which was "real" seemed larger, and what was real didn't always sell, so there was pressure from both sides of that divide: be real enough to stay underground, or go pop enough to get money. Tribe found themselves at the center of this tug-of-war, having already established an underground following, but with enough pop chops to get played on radio. There is selling out, and then there is simply being good enough to reach everyone at once.

Still, when Tip and Phife echo each other, insisting that they are both on point once again, it feels as if they are asking an audience to believe what they know is not true anymore of themselves or their relationship.

When people talk about *Beats, Rhymes and Life* now, it is labeled a grand failure—the beginning of a sharp and rapid decline that would end in the disbanding of Tribe just two years later, in the summer of 1998. Which isn't entirely accurate.

Because Tribe walked the commercial-underground line so well by 1996, and had already mastered catering to their underground roots, a tip in the opposite direction seemed inevitable and almost necessary. Still, between Consequence and Dilla's additions to the Tribe, the formula was noticeably off, as was Q-Tip and Phife's comfort within the new formula.

The production was clean but didn't exactly serve the group's needs very well. The addition of Consequence flourished in spots, like on the song "Stressed Out," for example. But in other spots, he was clunky and slowed down momentum. Despite being skilled, on a song like "Motivators," Consequence quite simply took up too much space, eagerly nestling in between Q-Tip's and Phife's verses to pull the track further and further away from the sharpness that Tribe had just seemed to get comfortable with. In many ways, Consequence's presence on the album acted like a wedge between the group's two MCs, holding each of them at arm's length. It's much easier to make that commentary now, of course, with the group's tensions during the making of the album well known. But even in the moment, when Consequence was on, he was effective, but when he was off, he was disruptive to the group's natural confidence and rhythm. Which makes sense, of course. He was brought in because the group was lacking the confidence and rhythm that had gotten them to this point.

Being good is only a failure if you've been impossible three times in a row. If you've carved new paths out of seemingly nothing, people might become confused when you don't do it again or when you veer into different territory that feels both new and uncomfortable rather than groundbreaking.

A Tribe Called Quest didn't fail with *Beats, Rhymes and Life*. The album had more than enough bright spots to not be a complete failure. While not as critically adored as their first three efforts, the album did get four stars from *Rolling Stone* and a four-mic rating from *The Source*. The problem was that, for the first time, A Tribe Called Quest made an album that didn't feel as though it was setting a pace for the genre. They made the album the genre wanted, not the album they wanted to see in the genre. And there's nothing wrong with that, really. But when you set a precedent on pushing forward, it's hard to simply be good.

"Baby Phife's Return" is a track of Phife's best rapping, buoyed by a Consequence hook. He's at his best on the song, pop culture and self-deprecation hidden under boasts:

Big up pop Duke, that's where I caught my athleticism
My mama, no doubt, that's where I got my lyricism
My nana, that's where I got my spiritualism
As for Tip and Shah, they made me stop from smokin' izm

In many ways, Phife is the star of the album, which is only interesting because of how disconnected he was from its creation. He runs a clinic on the productions, playing with breath and pace but remaining light on his feet. He steals the show on "The Pressure" and "The Hop," both comical and vicious in his rhymes, as in this excerpt from the latter:

You see you, your career is done like Johnny Carson's
Get me vexed, I do like Left Eye, start an arson
Now that I got that out my system
Watch me stab up the track as if my name was OJ Simpson
I packs it in like Van Halen
I work for mine, you, you're freeloading like Kato Kaelin

It makes sense that the album on which Q-Tip decided to take his hands slightly off the wheel was also the album where Phife shined the brightest, but it was also the album seen as a letdown to the general public. *Beats, Rhymes and Life* is an album of conflict, laid over a sonic calm. It is not a happy album. Gone are the upbeat crew cuts and the odes to ease and community. Instead it includes songs about depression, stresses of fame, and bemoaning the industry they were in. The very first track is "Phony Rappers," where Phife and Q-Tip trade stories about the decline of artistry in the game. The tone of the album feels very bitter and dark, reflecting a group no longer interested in uplifting their genre and more interested in performing an autopsy on it.

Still, *Beats, Rhymes and Life* was A Tribe Called Quest's first Number 1 album. It was long overdue for them to achieve commercial success, after being critical darlings for years. The album was certified gold, and then platinum. And this is how it works sometimes: when there is a crisis of faith, both musical and personal, the things we create become beloved, even though we know the interior of that creative process and want never to imagine being inside it again.

Just two months after *Beats, Rhymes and Life* was released, Tupac Shakur was dead. After a shooting in Las Vegas on the night of September 7, 1996, he was rushed to the hospital, where he eventually succumbed to his wounds on September 13. The feud that had been threatening to spill over for years finally had a high-profile death, marked with its name. Six months later, the Notorious B.I.G. was shot dead in Los Angeles while sitting in a parked car.

Few people talk about the time in between and the time immediately after the two deaths, but I remember distinctly thinking that it was over. Rap had had a good run, but now it needed to end, because blood was being shed, with no sign of when it would stop. It seemed to me that all of the white talking heads on the news were right. There was no turning back from this violence. No place that rap could go. This was extreme, of course. But the tensions in the coastal battle had hit the highest of breaking points, and it didn't seem like there was any direction the two sides could go in except for an all-out violence that canceled the music altogether.

I am saying there was a moment when I thought *Beats, Rhymes and Life* would be the final album A Tribe Called Quest ever made, and so I forced myself into loving it, believing I would never hear their voices again.

CHAPTER SEVEN

The Source **Cover**

If you were a resident of a home that cared about hip-hop in the 1980s and 1990s, your home probably got a monthly delivery of *The Source* magazine. And if your home didn't get it, you maybe knew the home of some other hip-hop fan who got it, and you maybe knew you could sneak off with it after they were done with their initial read. My brother kept his issues stacked in a corner, next to the large chest that held all his cassette tapes. Even in the nineties, when the CD player was becoming more and more prominent as the cost of one declined from the early to mid-1980s, allowing more CDs to be produced, my brother stuck with his loyalty to the cassette tape, influencing me to also develop a loyalty to the cassette tape. In all the ways people have listened to music over the past forty or fifty years, it can be argued that the cassette tape is the most tedious and least practical. It offers some of the same satisfaction as listening on vinyl: due to how difficult it is to skip songs, it makes the whole album listening experience vital—something worth celebrating. But the cassette is more fragile and less beloved when viewed through a lens of nostalgia. In the battered Walkman I owned, the tape inside the cassette would often get wound around one of the spokes inside the player, forcing the tape to unravel from the shell of the cassette. Countless tapes were ruined this way, by having to hand-wind the tape back into the cassette's plastic body, warping the insides and leaving a listener with a cacophony of only barely decipherable warbling.

But despite the fragility of the cassette, when I was young, I appreciated what it demanded from a listener. A cassette locked a listener into a commitment, particularly in the mid to late 1990s, when rap albums were sprawling, overrun with skits and Easter eggs. To skip a song could also mean you'd miss something. On Wu-Tang's 1993 *Enter the Wu-Tang (36 Chambers)*, for example, one would be wrong to pass over the skit before the song "Method Man," where Meth and Raekwon playfully spar over excruciating acts of torture; or in 1999, before MF Doom's "Hands of Doom," where two graffiti artists discuss Doom as a character, building out the ethos of both artist and persona in a few lines; or any of the children's storybook skits that littered the 1991 De La Soul album *De La Soul Is Dead*, creating a narrative around a young kid finding a De La Soul album in the garbage, only to have it stolen from him by bullies who listen to and critique the tape as the album unfolds, ending with them putting the album back in the same trash can where it was first found. The nuances of the album were part of the journey, so one had to endure whatever one must to take it all in.

The value of the tape was also the crafting of a mixtape. I am from an era when we learned not to waste songs. If you are creating a cassette that you must listen to all the way through, and you are crafting it with your own hands and your own ideas, then it is on you not to waste sounds and to structure a tape with feeling. No skippable songs meant that I wouldn't have to take my thick gloves off during the chill of a Midwest winter to hit fast-forward on a Walkman, hoping that I would stop a song just in time. No skippable songs meant that when the older, cooler kids on my bus ride to school asked what I was listening to in my headphones, armed with an onslaught of jokes if my shit wasn't on point, I could hand my head-phones over, give them a brief listen of something that would pass quality control, and keep myself safe from humiliation for another day.

The trick was recording from CD to cassette. Recording from cassette to cassette was an option, but only for the desper-ate, because the sound quality in that transfer would drop sig-nificantly. But if you had a good CD recorder—as we did in my house—you could set your tape to record songs straight from a compact disc, which not only improved sound quality but made for fewer abrupt stops in the process of recording. I would get CDs from the library near my house, which allowed you to take out five at a time in seven-day bursts. If you were particularly strapped for time or feeling especially confident about an artist or a group, you might just set the CD to record for the entire length of it, copying a whole album's worth of songs and then sorting them out later. When *Beats, Rhymes and Life* came out, for example, I remember recording it all the way through. By that time, Tribe had earned a type of currency that engendered that kind of trust. It was assumed that any album with their name on it would surely be worth its weight in gold, with no outright skippable songs. On each of their previous albums, even the less-than-great songs managed to be tolerable.

That trust fell apart on *Beats, Rhymes and Life*—which doesn't mean the album was bad so much as it means the album couldn't live up to the impossible standards of my own imagination. It sat in my Walkman during the winter of 1996, and I would pull my fingers out of gloves and rush to fast-forward what I could before the wind forced my hands back to the warmth they craved, and then I just stopped listening to it altogether.

While undergoing the task of making cassettes, I would often sit on the floor next to the stereo and read through the old issues of *The Source* that had accumulated over the years. The thing about *The Source*, in those days, was that it acted as a multilayered beacon for hip-hop culture. There was the unsigned hype column, which turned an eye toward acts that were underground but on the verge of breaking out. There were long, sprawling profiles of rappers that ranged from the delightfully absurd to the emotionally engaging and en-lightening. Every issue opened with the hip-hop quotable, highlighting the best rap verse from the past month. Before social media provided a platform for discourse, these would be debated in person, in parks during breaks between basketball games, in barbershops, or in basements. Also, *The Source* had covers that now seem comical but seemed brilliant at the time—covers that painted black rap stars as larger-than-life and sometimes heroic. Timbaland and Missy acting out a scene from *The Matrix*, or Puff Daddy hooked to a giant glowing machine, or Dr. Dre putting a revolver to his own head.

But what was more vital than all of this was *The Source*'s album review system. It was the first album review metric I ever knew, and one I came to rely on. It was simple: albums were rated on a scale of one to five mics. The one mic was as bad as it could get, and a five-mic album was a classic. *The Source* was known for its hardline, detailed reviews. They were unafraid to take a legend to task if that legend didn't live up to what they were capable of on an outing, like giving Slick Rick three mics on *Behind Bars* in 1995—an album he released while incarcerated, no less. *The Source* didn't deal in sympathy for circumstances. If an album was to climb the mountain and achieve the heralded five-mic status, it had to be a classic, not just on its first listen but also on its fifth. It had to be the kind of tape you could put in a Walkman and know that you would not need to skip a single song. *The Source* reviews were a way of life, with the "five mic" vernacular working its way into language used elsewhere, to describe anything that was fresh. It helped that *The Source* was stingy with its five-mic reviews in its early days. They would get close with many albums, giving out the 4.5-mic review almost as a tease and debate starter. But over the magazine's first ten years, from 1988 to 1998, it only gave out five-mic reviews to nine albums total, with four of them coming in 1990 alone. The albums bestowed the honor of the five-mic review within that first ten-year window were as follows:

> *Let the Rhythm Hit 'Em*—Eric B. and Rakim
> *AmeriKKKa's Most Wanted*—Ice Cube
> *One for All*—Brand Nubian
> *De La Soul Is Dead*—De La Soul
> *Illmatic*—Nas
> *Life After Death*—The Notorious B.I.G.
> *Aquemini*—Outkast

The other two were two albums by A Tribe Called Quest: *People's Instinctive Travels* and *The Low End Theory* both secured the honor, making A Tribe Called Quest the first act ever to have two five-mic albums awarded by the magazine. Later, when the magazine went back to rerate albums that they either didn't get to upon their release or that they felt deserved a rating adjustment, others like Ice Cube and Run-DMC were rightly added to that group. But early on, it was just A Tribe Called Quest, alone at the top of the mountain with a hand on each masterpiece.

In October of 1998, the cover of *The Source* sent especially jarring shockwaves through the communities it landed in. Against a soft blue background, all three members of A Tribe Called Quest are cloaked in black. To the right is Phife Dawg, round sunglasses atop a head full of waves, looking at the ground. On the left, also looking at the ground is Ali Shaheed Muhammad, somehow looking even more morose than Phife, his lip protruding slightly. In the center is Q-Tip, the only one looking straight at the camera, but through a low hat, his head bowed slightly, his eyes fixated on the cameras lens—one of the few white things in the shot. It is a piercing photo. Even if one didn't read the words below the picture, it would be obvious to anyone holding the cover that something had gone or was going awry. The words below the picture confirmed every worst fear: "Exclusive Interview: BREAK UP! A Tribe Called Quest Disbands."

I suppose there is something to be missed about a print magazine breaking big news. I'm not sure if that could happen now. The internet existed in 1998, of course, but not in the way it existed after 2009 or so, when the accessibility of breaking news seemed to be almost too much—something that many would likely say is absolutely true now, nearly a decade later. In 1998, the rap media landscape was also different. *Yo! MTV Raps* had been gone for three years already, and BET's *Rap City*—certainly a worthwhile show—was in a state of transition, bringing in new hosts and moving on from the earlier ones. If one of the biggest rap groups in the world wanted to announce their disbandment in a way that would reach the rap world quickly and with the right level of weight, they would do it in the biggest print rap magazine there was at the time. It gives me a type of comfort, like hearing a cassette player click when it reaches the end of a really satisfying tape.

One of the only other magazines that arrived at my childhood house was *Jet*. *Jet* was a legacy black publication, the kind of magazine that any black person could find in almost any other black person's home. It was almost a test: you go into a black person's home and look around, and before you know it, there's a *Jet* magazine on the kitchen table, or in the bathroom, or on a tray next to some hard peppermint candies. It's tough to say who had the subscription to *Jet* in my home. It often felt like a subscription to the magazine was something passed down though generations. *Jet* was started in 1951 by John Harold Johnson, who was the grandson of slaves and who loved learning so much that he once repeated the eighth grade in rural Arkansas just to stay in school, since there were not yet high schools that black people could go to. His family eventually moved to Chicago, where there were more opportunities for schooling and work for black people. After high school, Johnson worked for Harry Pace at the Supreme Life Insurance Company. Part of his duties included making a small weekly newspaper to circulate among the staff and in surrounding neighborhoods. With an eye for engaging audiences of readers and a small window into how the publishing world worked, he dreamed up an idea of publishing magazines. The first, *Black Digest*, he set up in 1942. He used his mother's furniture as collateral and secured a $500 loan.

Of all the sacrifices of black motherhood, I imagine this to be among the highest, in some ways. The Johnson family grew up poor, with little to their name. In *The Bluest Eye*, Toni Morrison talks about the pride the Breedlove family has in their couches—the way these things can be symbols for a people who don't have much but own the little they do have, and own it as a result of their own pained labor. I do not know what had earned John Harold Johnson's mother her furniture, but she was willing to risk her ownership of it for her ambitious son. And so it was.

Black Digest was changed to *Negro Digest* before its first publication, and then eventually to *Black World*. In 1945, Johnson used the slight momentum and trust he had gained to start *Ebony* magazine, which took off, regularly selling out of its 25,000-copy run. What Johnson knew was simple: when these magazines took off, black people not only *wanted* to see positive images of themselves, they *needed* to see positive images of themselves. It was the right magazine at the right time. Many living black people in the early to mid-1940s were like Johnson and his family: children and grandchildren of slaves. The historical impacts of slavery were still echoing far and wide throughout parts of the country, particularly in the southern states. *Ebony*, in its initial stages, offered full-color photos of successful black people, along with photo essays and glamorous ads with black people in them. It wasn't a magazine that could save the world or any black people in it, but it did offer a small glimpse into a better possibility—a window of some dreams being fulfilled in a place that might not be your place, but a place where someone who looks like you is living a little better, and you could live through them.

All of *Ebony*'s success allowed for Johnson to pursue *Jet* magazine in 1951. *Jet*'s initial aims were a bit different from *Ebony*'s, in that Johnson wanted the magazine to lean heavier into the roots of a digest. It was released weekly, and the magazine itself was small in shape. In the first issue, Johnson stated: "In the world today everything is moving along at a faster clip. There is more news and far less time to read it."

Jet became notable for how much it could fit into an issue. The magazine contained fashion tips, entertainment and television news, politics, and—starting in 1952—the Beauty of the Week, usually the final page in the magazine.

In our home, *Jet* magazine would sit in our bathroom, on the back of the toilet. Because they accumulated at a weekly clip, finding a space in your home to hold all of them throughout the year became tricky. Cycling through a month or two in stacks behind the toilet seemed as good a way to do this as any. The Beauty of the Week was the closest anyone in my house could get to print magazine indecency. I didn't grow up in a house where one might stumble upon their father's stash of *Playboy* magazines or VHS tapes of porn. *Jet*, for all of its historical weight and cultural relevance, also provided a place for a curious kid to see beautiful black women every week. In retrospect, Beauty of the Week was a bit archaic—even though it wasn't just a woman in a bikini, as it also offered facts about her life—but at the time, it was serving a similar purpose that all black magazines had served throughout their history: a window into desire.

Jet was also known for its relevance in covering the civil rights movement when few other places would. The most infamous case of this came in 1955, when *Jet* sent reporters to the funeral of Emmett Till. The coverage of his funeral included the now-infamous picture of his horribly disfigured body, swollen, beaten, and water-logged. *Jet* chose to run the images uncensored. The images also managed to capture Emmett's mother, Mamie Till, looking stoically upon her son's body. Mamie wanted to have an open-casket funeral as a way of reflecting the world's horror back onto itself. *Jet* felt a duty to amplify this. And so, in every home and on every newsstand within *Jet*'s circulation, there was the picture of Emmett Till's remains. The photo created an urgency around a movement. The things black people had been experiencing and trying to tell the world about were presented, right there, for everyone to see. A worthwhile reason to fight back emerged. The casket was always going to be open, as Mamie Till wished. But it was *Jet*'s ability to capture the moment that made the funeral echo through generations.

A somewhat shakier judgment call occurred a little over a decade later. Fewer people mention this when they mention *Jet* and the legacy of black magazines using stark imagery to provoke readers. In December of 1967, *Jet* ran another stunning photo of the dead. Otis Redding died in a plane crash on December 10, drowning and freezing to death in Wisconsin's Lake Monona. Redding, still strapped to his seat and stuck, couldn't free himself, and so he drowned. He had to be pulled from the depths of the lake, and when he was finally pulled up, he was frozen, dead in his seat.

Jet ran the photo of Otis Redding in this way. It is a haunting and terrifying image, Redding, frozen and stiff. *Jet*'s decision to run the photo was met with significantly more criticism from the black community than their decision to run the Till photo. Many saw it as craven and aimless, without any call to action behind it, or thoughtfulness about how it might impact people. And so, in the homes of black families and on news-stands in black neighborhoods, there was the photo of an icon, immovable, teeming with frozen blood.

Otis Redding should probably have never taken off with that plane in the first place, but isn't that how all stories like this one start? It was raining and foggy, and the winter weather didn't bode well for travel, especially on the route being taken. Otis was traveling with the Bar-Kays, a soul and funk group that Otis heard in Memphis and chose as his backing band. The group was traveling from Cleveland, Ohio, to a gig near Madison, Wisconsin, where the fog was increasing by the hour and the temperature was dropping.

When I think about the Otis Redding plane crash—especially in the context of this story—I don't think about the deaths. I think about the one person who lived. It was never determined why exactly the plane went down, but when it was less than four miles away from its destination, it began a plunge into the icy waters of the lake.

Ben Cauley was the most notable member of the Bar-Kays because, if nothing else, he was the best dressed. He was always in a pressed suit, no matter the occasion. He was also arguably the best looking and one of the most talented members of the group, his trumpet skills equally matched by his vocal ability and songwriting chops. The Bar-Kays operated in such a way that they didn't have a single bandleader, but the bulk of their creative output fell on Cauley, who embraced the challenge.

Ben Cauley was asleep when the plane began its plummet from the Wisconsin sky. He was jarred awake when he realized that he couldn't breathe, due to the air pressure dropping. Cauley had fallen asleep directly behind Redding earlier in the flight, holding his seat cushion to his chest. When he woke, he looked over and saw his bandmate Phalon Jones looking out of a window and yelling "Oh no!"

Cauley instinctively unbuckled his seatbelt. It seems like such an odd thing to do as a plane you are in careens toward the ground, but I imagine it is a question of what our instincts tell us about getting free. Sometimes it is just the single thing. Cauley, unbuckled from his seat, was able to float away from the wreckage, still clutching his seat cushion, which he used to float above the water. No one in the plane could swim, and even if they could have, it wouldn't have mattered. Everyone else was still attached to their seats, unable to free themselves in their panic. Since Cauley couldn't swim, he couldn't offer any assistance to his friends and bandmates. They screamed his name and yelled for help as the frigid water pulled them under, and he watched, helpless.

This is what a picture in a magazine couldn't capture. The often-untold story about Otis Redding's death is all about what it is to be unable to save the people you love, even though you want to. It's a question of choosing to save yourself first over choosing to save everyone else. Ben Cauley said he never stopped having nightmares about the crash, right up until he died in 2015. He reformed the Bar-Kays after the crash but left the group in 1971. He lived the vast majority of his life tortured by what he couldn't do. It's likely he closed his eyes every night and heard the screams of the people he couldn't save.

It is funny—all the ways we use drowning as a metaphor.

The Love Movement was the final Tribe Called Quest album,

though no one knew that when it came out. It was released on September 29, 1998, just before *The Source* cover came out. The album got somewhat mixed reviews at the point of its release, and the reviews became more mixed as the news of the group's dismantling surfaced. The lack of satisfaction people had was with the idea that we were given one final, unsatisfying Tribe album—one that came close to the sound of their first three efforts but not close enough. Phife's verses sounded lazy and half-hearted, save for a few bright moments, like on "Busta's Lament," where he shines in a brief burst, and then he's gone. Especially for people who thought *Beats, Rhymes and Life* was a turn toward a more commercial sound, *The Love Movement* seemed to complete that trajectory. "Commercial" is somewhat of an unfair assessment, as Tribe still wasn't making music that could get tons of radio spins. But it felt like the ease with which they approached their past efforts was out the window.

In a 4-out-of-10 review, *Spin* writer Tim Haslett wrote of the album: "Toni Morrison once said of black art that it must look effortless. If it makes you sweat, you haven't done the work. *The Love Movement* finds A Tribe Called Quest with sweat filling their palms." In a mixed review from the *A.V. Club*, Nathan Rabin wrote: "Unfortunately, *The Love Movement* replicates the sound of *Beats, Rhymes And Life* so thoroughly that it might as well be titled *More Beats, More Rhymes And Even More Life*."

And this was the way of it. A Tribe Called Quest wanted to go out on a concept album about love, but the only problem was that they didn't love each other, and it didn't seem as if they loved the world they were occupying anymore. The result was a tedious, seemingly joyless album. It didn't help that 1998 was one of rap's greatest, most sonically diverse years. Two other albums were released on September 29, 1998: Jay-Z's *Vol. 2 . . . Hard Knock Life* and Outkast's *Aquemini*. Even with the promise of Tribe hanging it up after *The Love Movement*, the album was quickly forgotten and found itself hard-pressed to keep pace with the other albums released around it—particularly *Aquemini*, which saw Outkast at the peak of their trajectory as the new, infallible hip-hop group. Outkast were just entering the period when the critics began to call them hip-hop's answer to the Beatles. Their sounds came from the South but spread everywhere. Their songs sat in a listener's bones and forced a bounce out of them. The members of the group were comical and eccentric, and they could *really* rap. Outkast made the hyperserious focus of Tribe—particularly Q-Tip—seem archaic. The two albums, when contrasted, felt like listening to what rap was, and then what rap was becoming.

I purchased both on cassette the day they came out, even though CDs were by then truly all the rage. I listened to *The Love Movement* longingly on a school bus in the early fall in Ohio, where the leaves began to fight against their inevitable departure. By the tree that hung over my bus stop, the leaves slowly began to gather around the tree's base, as if to say *We did our best. We'll try again next time.*

It is really hard coming to terms with watching something not have any fight left. It's not that A Tribe Called Quest couldn't have continued to be great and attempt great things, and it is not that the sound in hip-hop was shifting so drastically that they couldn't have found a lane. Sure, my pals and I stopped being fascinated with the jazz hybridity when our parents stopped giving a fuck that we were sneaking rap albums into the house. But A Tribe Called Quest could still have had a niche, even with groups like Outkast and labels like No Limit and Cash Money Records starting a trajectory of southern chart dominance. The problem was that A Tribe Called Quest simply didn't have it in them to fight anymore. They built the whole tree, and held on to it for as long as they could, and then their season arrived, and they decided to drift down and make their peace with falling.

Every group of two or more musicians often has a clear leader, and here it is the one who could stand to look into the camera when the photographer had the other members of the group look away. Here, it is the one who stood in the center of the photo to absorb the full weight of whatever came next. I blamed Q-Tip for a long time. I stayed angry at him the way someone might stay angry at a loved one who abandons them and takes the whole home with them when they leave. I figured it must have been Q-Tip's wild ambition that pulled the group apart and nothing else. For years, this was the narrative sold. Q-Tip was the genius of the Native Tongues collective. Beyond the brilliance of Monie Love, the Jungle Brothers, even beyond the brilliance of De La Soul and Queen Latifah, there was Q-Tip.

It helps that he was a visionary and that he was ambitious, and it helps that he couldn't fathom failure as an option for A Tribe Called Quest, which did lead to him dragging the band along to and through his vision, no matter what it was.

But it was easy for me to blame Q-Tip, flawed as the premise might have been. I imagined the toll his relentless vision may have taken on everyone else around him. I remembered a shot from a *Yo! MTV Raps* interview in 1991: in a hallway, A Tribe Called Quest is being interviewed before they go on stage. Q-Tip has his arms around host Fab Five Freddy, eagerly rapping into his mic while Ali Shaheed Muhammad holds another mic in Q-Tip's face. Q-Tip is energetic, talking with excitement about the group's tour and album, while Phife, walking several steps ahead, stares blankly into space, almost invisible to the viewer.

There is more to it than this, of course. Q-Tip and Phife had a complex relationship, made more complex by the fact that they had known each other for their entire lives—since the age of two years old. What is hard to do is imagine a world in which someone you have loved—before you knew what love is—has to balance that love with whatever ambitions they have for a journey you set out on together. I don't know what it was like for Q-Tip to have to fight to get Phife into the studio during the first few albums, and I don't know what it was like for Phife to feel that he wasn't able to get any creative control of the vision *he* had for the group and its music. But I know that sometimes you have to pull away from your brother in order for you to keep looking at him like he is your brother.

I stopped blaming Q-Tip nearly a year after the group broke up, when it became clear that they weren't getting back together. The two hardly spoke of each other, and they didn't seem too interested in being in the same worlds anymore. It was both tragic and understandable.

In my bedroom, I went through a phase where I cut out pictures from magazines, or tore old magazine covers off and taped them to my wall. This was in the early 2000s, when magazine covers were arguably at their best and most absurd. By that time, I had subscribed to *ESPN the Magazine* and *Slam* magazine, and *XXL* magazine came to my house. Everyone on every cover was larger than life, plastered against some wild background or paired with some animal: Ma$e with a tiger or basketball player Kevin Garnett with a wolf. It's like the magazines catering to black people finally had the eyes and resources and capital to catch up with what *Rolling Stone* had been doing with covers for decades.

I hung the old Tribe cover of *The Source* somewhere above my bed. I'm reminded of how black magazines lean first on sight before trying to stimulate any of the other senses. A small magazine started by one black man and some furniture as collateral started a movement once, they say. They don't all do that, of course. But sometimes they provide an image that haunts you, be it a frozen soul icon or the whites of Q-Tip's eyes against so much darkness. Asking for forgiveness, maybe, but still with a bit of hope. As if he'd grown tired of watching everything he built drown slowly, and decided to finally stop fighting against the water and trying to save it.

CHAPTER EIGHT

Lament

DEAR PHIFE,

Do you know that it wasn't the ball trickling through Bill Buckner's legs that lost the Red Sox the 1986 World Series? It's funny, isn't it—the things that play on our screens and in our heads for years, detached from any fullness. Maybe you remember this. It helped deliver a World Series to your beloved Queens. But I'm going to talk to you for a second like you don't remember. I'm going to talk to you like this isn't about facts, but about memory.

Bill Buckner should maybe not even have been on the field for that game six. Bill Buckner was an All-Star once, in 1981. My college roommate had a dad who loved Bill Buckner. Or maybe my college roommate had a dad who felt sorry for Bill Buckner. I'm always thinking about the distance between love and sympathy, Phife. How quickly one can feel like the other in the right light, or in the right season, or with the right song acting as its anchor. But this isn't about love. I'm saying that I, too, felt bad for Bill Buckner once, because I thought he lost an entire city its closest hope at a World Series. This was before the 2000s, when the Red Sox won it all and became dominant. This was when there was still talk of the curse, and we know how it is with sports and scapegoats.

Earlier that year, in January of 1986, the temperature in South Florida unexpectedly dropped to twenty degrees overnight. This would have been an unspectacular flash of weather if not for an O-ring attached to the *Challenger* space shuttle. The rings were designed to keep pressurized hydrogen out of the rocket boosters, and because the shuttle was launching from Florida, engineers stopped just short of testing to see if the O-rings would function in cold weather. The O-ring, as it turns out, stopped functioning at any temperature below forty degrees. The *Challenger*, seventy-three seconds into its flight, converted into a bomb, killing everyone on board. If Florida hadn't had a record-low morning, or if one engineer would have thought to test at any temperature below forty degrees, the *Challenger* is a success story instead of a tragedy.

What I'm saying, Phife, is that sometimes, it's just the one thing. In life, but rarely in sports. In sports, it's the melting pot of several things, boiled down into one digestible highlight of a thing. In the 1986 World Series, Bill Buckner was batting .143. He was 0 for 5 in game six, before the ball rolled through his legs. He had been failing on defense throughout the series. Dave Stapleton had been coming in as his defensive replacement in the later innings all playoffs long, but for some reason, that didn't happen here. When the game went into extra innings, Buckner was still in the game.

You know how this goes, Phife. Everything is a game of small movements—of jolts and bumps and unexpected turns. A baseball is thrown at one hundred miles an hour, and then comes off a bat, speeding along uneven ground. In the moment, anything can take a player briefly away from their focus. The thought of someone they love, the idea of being a hero before completing the heroic task, the fear of what might befall them if they don't complete said task. It's all so impossible to keep up with. I don't blame Bill Buckner as much as I blame the impossibility of the moments so many of us are asked to rise to, when we would likely be better off playing catch in the backyard or kicking freestyles with our brothers in the basement inside a home where we first heard the songs our parents sang falling from their mouths while a record played.

It was game six, anyway. No one ever mentions that part, do they? I get it. I know. It's easier to point at the one thing. But it's never just the one thing in sports. Even if Buckner would have executed the play, the game would have simply gone to another inning, and then who knows, right? I'm saying that I'm an optimist, overwhelmed with sympathy for those who touched the hem of greatness but then let it slip through their fingers. Bill Buckner was 2 for 4 in game seven and scored a run. But it didn't matter. New York still won. No one talks about game seven, though. But I'm sure you knew that. Maybe you were a kid who celebrated the Mets winning a World Series and maybe you threw back your head to laugh at the misfortune of Bill Buckner, as I would have if I were in Queens, New York, and young, and a lover of sports as you were. We take what we can where we can, Phife. I guess that's what I'm saying. I guess I'm saying mercy is something I've reserved for even the people who surely don't need it from me, and I'm wondering if you've ever done the same.

I heard the album that no one listened to and I played it over and over again during the fall of 2000. I got it, Phife. *Ventilation: Da LP*. You had things to get off your chest, and who wouldn't? You were done being the punch-line-heavy comedic foil of a group that you felt distant from, finally. I loved that on the cover you wore a Jets jersey with your name on the back, because it was the early 2000s when everyone wore jerseys, and the Jets had the best ones in the game. I loved how bitter you sounded, Phife. I always wanted you to sound like you wanted to prove yourself again. I get that you thought you didn't get your shine, and I believed you then, and I believed you always. I saw you in the interviews, sometimes bursting at your edges to speak, only to be drowned out. I saw you in photos, playing the background. What you gave in song was so much larger than what you were asked to give outside of it. I was thankful for your anger, Malik. I played *Ventilation* for my friends who loved Tribe but didn't believe any of you could make it on your own, and none of them believed in you, but I did. You only get to be the underdog once, you know. You only get to fight back from something that seems insurmountable one good time before people get tired of seeing you do it, and I loved you for trying. I loved you the way I loved my hand, balled into a tight fist and thrown at the jaw of a bully in my ninth grade year, the year my older and bigger brother and I weren't at the same school and I became a target. I loved you the way I loved the way the grass felt as I fell to my knees after upsetting the greatest high school soccer team in my league when I was a senior, nearly a year after *Ventilation* had come and gone.

I don't know why people did not love your solo album, Phife, but I did. I loved the soaring and swooning production, and I loved how focused you sounded on it. It is easy to pretend now that you were never interesting enough to sustain a solo career, but we both know that's a lie. And maybe I was just always cheering for you because, in some ways, cheering for you felt like cheering for myself. And we both needed that.

Phife, it is late now, in a whole other year beyond the one where you gave the world your album, and I can't find it anywhere. They took it out of print, and I wish I knew why. I found it in an old CD shop in New York once, and they were selling it for $30. When I talk to people about it now, no one remembers it, or talks about it the way I did when I spent an entire season playing it from start to finish. I think a lot about what it means to take an album out of print, and how it erases a small part of an artist's past. And this was it for you—your big payback, the loudest thing you made, which no one heard.

The term "commercial failure" is only the tip of the iceberg, and the rest is not built so well underneath. You get what I'm saying now, Phife. You and I, we're sports fans. We know all the drama and narrative of success and failure and wins and losses. *Ventilation* is the ball that skipped through your legs, but it was never your fault. You were at the mercy of unfair machinery, the same way Bill Buckner was at the mercy of an unpredictable and unforgiving plot of land, and a ball that decided its own destiny.

But I think fools believe in curses, don't you? Some teams are just bad, some shots just miss, and some albums just aren't met with the hands they deserve to be met with.

But people only remember the big things, the things they can point at—in joy or in some type of defeat. Here's another one that I know you know already, Phife, but I am going to talk to you like you maybe don't remember, because some people out there don't, and I'm talking to them as much as I'm talking to you, anyway.

When Willis Reed limped out onto the court in the 1970 NBA Finals, the game seven was perhaps already won for your beloved Knicks. Willis Reed only played the first half, though, scoring two buckets and harassing Wilt Chamberlain into a bad offensive outing. But what won the game was Willis Reed limping onto the court. That's all people remember. That's all people talk about. That's the bright thing that people point at, and it almost doesn't even matter what Reed's statistics were. He came out on a bad leg and stood, and that was good enough.

I don't know where you are or what you are doing these days, but I do hope that you'll find a tunnel to limp out of soon, Phife. I do hope that we remember you always for your fight and not your failure. I paid $30 for the old copy of *Ventilation* that I found in that New York CD shop, because I didn't know if I'd ever find a copy again, and I refuse to let that album die. I'll still play it for people who think that you didn't have a solo career worth celebrating, just because no one was there to call you a genius. Some will remember it as the ball going through your legs, but I'll remember it as you limping out of the tunnel and standing.

I know you get where I'm coming from. We're sports fans, you and I.

DEAR ALI SHAHEED MUHAMMAD,

You will be pleased to know that we did in fact dance to Lucy Pearl underneath the fluorescent lights of Beechcroft High School's gym during a lunch period sock hop that had no business taking place in an afternoon when some of us had to get back to class right after, but we did it anyway. There is something about showing up in a place of learning with fresh sweat sitting on your skin from the flailing of your body up against something as immovable as a school day with more school left on the other side of your flailing.

Did you ever think people would dance to you anywhere you crawled out of a speaker? There's something black about this urgency, sure. But I must imagine you saw it, perhaps in a dream. Wherever there is a day when people are living, there might not be one after it, and so I will not waste the capabilities my legs still have, you know?

It was the song "Dance Tonight," and I recall this because I have never heard it again as I did in that moment and, Ali, I was an awkward and nervous kid and I maybe could not dance as well as I thought I could dance (but who can?), and it was the end of the 1990s and I had never kissed a girl I actually liked, and when I say fluorescent lights, what I really mean is that someone turned out all the lights in the auditorium and dragged in a couple of stage lights from the spring production of *Romeo and Juliet*, and our drama teacher was really mad about it, but by the time he found out, the song was already being played on repeat for its third time and there are some parties you just don't want to stop, even if they are being built on the back of the things you consider sacred.

I kissed someone I liked during the fourth time I heard the first verse, and she liked me back—or at least she liked me back in that moment. I'm saying that you built a world for me then, like you always did. What I have always loved about you, Ali, is that you were a builder of soft spaces for anyone who needed them. What you never got enough credit for was the way you made even silence a commodity.

I kissed someone I liked during the first verse of "Dance Tonight," which I was hearing for the fourth time in a row, and I retreated to a classroom that afternoon, baptized in sweat and whatever a teenager imagines as love, and I let the song rattle around in my head for hours, tied to the end of countless possibilities.

And you maybe don't need to know that the girl I kissed transferred schools shortly thereafter and we never saw each other again, and maybe the kiss was both of us having the idea of taking a big risk before the world as we knew it changed. But I'm telling you that anyway, and I'm telling you so that you know every time I hear that song I think of a moment when I was not afraid. I think of a moment when I truly escaped into the urgency that it was pulling from me. It's a song that demands that. It's a song that asks us to do what we might do if we knew we were going to die the next day.

Ali, what was it about Dawn Robinson that made all of us fall for her, and did you fall, as I did? As your brother Phife did when he rapped *I used to have a crush on Dawn from En Vogue* in "Oh My God?" It's funny how things come full circle like this, without our even knowing. In the video for "Dance Tonight," there is Dawn, dancing in a room full of dancers and still making it look effortless. In the video for "Don't Mess with My Man," there is Dawn again. There are all of you, actually. Sweaty, but just the right amount of sweaty. The kind that doesn't seem like it would be uncomfortable during a rooftop party at the end of summer. And here I was, wanting Lucy Pearl to never end. I heard the story once about how D'Angelo was supposed to be in the band instead of Dawn, but no. I think the Gods got this one right. Something echoed down and got this one as right as it could ever have been.

Speaking of our Gods. My middle name is Muhammad—the same name that anchors your own. I sometimes thought it was because my parents ran out of cool ideas after having three children before me. I am saddled with the name of the Prophet, as you are. As many are. What a way to be part of a religion—to have yourself named after the greatest prophet the faith has to offer.

Of all the stories we hear in Muslim households—and I'm sure you've heard as many as I have, if not more—the one I return to most is the story of the Archangel Gabriel coming to Muhammad and demanding that he read. He couldn't read, but the angel held him close and demanded again that he read, and the words just came to him, like they had been there all along. I don't know where you are with your faith or if you, like me, have spent countless days, hours, and months praying and losing hope and then finding it somewhere else. But I don't know if I'm talking about faith or God here as much as I'm talking about what it is to offer someone sight where there was no sight.

I wonder if you listen to things with your eyes closed sometimes, as I do. I am wondering if in the summer, you climb to the rooftops and put on headphones and let a world be built around you, a world better than whatever one you're currently in. I open my windows in summer and let the breeze in while music plays. Last summer, it was hot, and not the romantic kind of hot. It was the kind of hot where you sweat and the sweat comes on heavy the minute you step out of the door. But I still opened my windows one night and just let the sweat arrive. I played the Lucy Pearl album. It's a relic now, but you should know that when I closed my eyes, I still saw everything just as I think you intended it. It was all blue. Everything hanging under some stolen lights made newly fluorescent. A room so packed that no one could move but for their frantic dancing.

I'm saying there's a language for this that I never quite understood but for you showing it to me. I hope whatever path you take leads you back to the arms of Tribe, but even if it never does, you've found a way to make a world again. You've found a way to give someone like me a place to land this time, and it wasn't just in a high school gym, but also in the open mouth of a window in a summer when it was too hot to breathe. Lucy Pearl was a feeling, Ali. I imagine you first as the angel that held me close and asked me to read when I could not see the words for myself. I imagine you first as the person who guided my hand, who guided the language onto my tongue.

Q-TIP,

I am glad it was not you that we lost in the fire, though records are also worth mourning. When I first read the story of the fire at the end of the 1990s, I thought of how impossible it seemed for any one person to own twenty thousand records. But I'd heard this about you—how you dug through all of the sounds you could possibly find to make your own brand of magic. I imagine it was the unreleased songs that hurt most. It was early 1998, and I'm sure you already knew that Tribe was going to be finished. I imagine you knew before the rest of us did. But the foolish among us were still holding out hope that you all would be together forever.

Everyone uses the same metaphor about fire: how those immersed in it rise from the ashes newer and sometimes better. It's tired, to be sure. But it works here. How you—with no records to sample—learned to make the music you had been hearing in your head the whole time. You learned to translate the beating on the table from the school where you and Phife were once young.

What didn't satisfy people about you is that your brand of genius never trended as close to madness as we're used to seeing, or that people want to see. Everyone wants a performance from the people they consider to be brilliant. Everyone wants the genius to eventually fall apart as a penance, some punishment for getting too close to the sun. You just worked harder than anyone else. Sometimes, it's a gift passed down from somewhere holy, and sometimes it's just hard work, and sometimes it's both. I don't know the toll it takes to keep a group alive past their expiration date. To drag people to the studio when they don't want to be there. To ask people to hear things that only you can hear. I'm sorry if I never gave you enough credit for that. I'm sorry that in the months after Tribe went away, I stayed mad at you, as if you could hold my anger in your hands and feel it from miles away. I'm sorry I blamed you for talking too much in interviews with the group, and for making Phife feel small. I think you maybe earned everything. But I hope you can understand wanting someone to blame for watching the greatness of an entire childhood slip through your fingers.

Tip, I must also admit that I found myself mad again when I heard your first offering, and I found myself mad again when I watched the video for said offering—drenched in black and white, half-naked women dancing on top of cars. Everyone I knew thought we'd lost you when *Amplified* came out in 1999, you on the cover with your arms stretched out wide with a silver shiny jacket adorning your shirtless body. I get it. It was the 1990s, and Big was gone and Tupac was gone and Big L was gone, and all white people could talk about was blood and bullets. Maybe you put away your records and decided to party for a while. To grab J Dilla by the collar and get him to lay down some drums motherfuckers could dance to.

I miss Dilla, Tip. Don't you? Don't you hear him sometimes when you close your eyes at night, as I do? If I could have one more year of him, I'd trade one hundred of our finest geniuses. But not you, Tip. Did you know that Dilla went to the same hospital to die as Biggie did? Did you know that inside his hospital room he rebuilt an entire studio so that he could finish *Donuts*? Did you know the story of his mother? How, when his hands were swollen and in pain from the disease taking over his body, she would massage them until the swelling went down so that he could finish working on the album? And, oh, what a joy *Donuts* was for us, Tip. How Dilla gave it to us with one hand, and then climbed his way to heaven with the other. I'm sure you knew all of this. I'm talking to you like maybe you didn't.

I want you to know that I no longer determine genius by how much pain someone can endure, and I owe Dilla for that, and you owe Dilla for so much more. I wanted you two to have another run at something, Tip. I wanted you both to create something that I could receive in a season where I felt nothing for you but a deep and abiding gratitude.

I heard Arista shelved your album back in 2002 because they didn't think it would hold up commercially, and can you believe that? This is why geniuses have to die first, I guess. I'm sorry that somewhere, someone behind a desk lost faith in you. I'm sorry that somewhere there are no horns or maybe no drums, or maybe somewhere there is a house on fire with every record that someone owns on the inside while they watch from a street where they can see the notes of all the music they love drifting into the air.

I'm not going to ask you to bring A Tribe Called Quest back. I read somewhere that you're working on something new—a *return to form*, the magazines say. Tip, did you ever listen to Phife's album? The solo album that no one bought and the one we were told no one listened to? I listened to it, Tip. It occurs to me now, all these years later, that he was maybe writing to you the whole time. Not as an apology—but just to show you how great he was all along. Do you know what it's like to be a little brother? You're always proving yourself, even when you think you're not. I've started to wonder if no one loved Phife's album because it was a love letter only to you and no one else. I want to know if you listened to it then, and I want to know if you still listen to it now. I want to know if you're as proud of him as I was. You don't have to tell him out loud, but I wish I could see the faintest smile spread across your face at the first opening of your brother's rhymes, Tip. I hope you aren't mad anymore, and I hope he's not mad anymore, and I hope you can forgive me for being mad once, but never again.

I once balled up a small fist and swung it as hard as I could at my older brother's face. Not because I wanted to hurt him, but because I wanted him to imagine a world in which I was unafraid to hurt him. There is a difference there—between wanting to harm someone and wanting to be feared. The part of the story that I don't tell is that after I hit my brother—after the punch danced across his face and left a small red mark—I ran away and locked myself in a closet while he seethed with rage. I made myself small in a corner with a pile of dirty clothes. I held my knees to my chest and I wept, and I am not sure why. I was maybe afraid. Not of the consequences, but of the brand-new knowledge of what my fists were capable of. If we are blessed with working hands at our birth, we then spend our lives making them into the machines we want them to be.

What I'm mostly saying, Tip, is that I'm glad we didn't lose you in the fire. I'm glad it was only music and a few songs and nothing else. I'm glad you learned how to rebuild, time and time again.

What I'm mostly saying, Tip, is that I haven't thrown a punch in years. The last time I did, I left a small brown mark in a white wall, and I swear the only sound that echoed back was the sound of something you made with your bare hands.

CHAPTER NINE

Documentary

The documentary surely seemed like a good idea. *Beats, Rhymes & Life: The Travels of A Tribe Called Quest* was a documentary released in 2011. It was helmed by actor and first-time director Michael Rapaport. Rapaport was a longtime Tribe fan who thought there was no reason not to attempt to put a film together. Even in 2011, thirteen years after the group's final album, there was still interest in them. If anything, the interest had heightened. They'd been gone so long, with only Q-Tip remaining very publicly active in music spaces over a consistent period during that time. The group, then, became seen as almost mythical. Their run in the early nineties was so distant but still something that was talked about, as if you had to have been there to fully appreciate it. Because their sound was so ahead of its time and concerned with pushing the boundaries of the spaces it was in, they made more sense in 2011, when the intricacies of multiple samples and a smoother sound template were seeping back into rap. Their old albums were being cited by rap's new stars as albums that offered a way into the genre. And so, with that, younger rap fans were getting hip to them and sticking around.

Moreover, Tribe became a staple around the discussion about what "real" hip-hop was. This discussion becomes more common with each passing year, as hip-hop heads of a certain era age, and the genre becomes more watered down—something that happens to every genre of music as it gets older. Tribe's music became a weapon—which was happening even before they split—used in opposition to the shiny suits, and then in opposition to more hardcore rap, and then in opposition to rap that people deemed to have no substance.

People talked about Tribe like they weren't real, which they weren't. Kind of. There would be Tribe sightings: headlining a festival in San Diego in 2004, or in a run of concerts in 2006, or headlining the Rock the Bells festival in both 2008 and 2011. Through all of this, however, there was never an understanding that the group was reunited. They were doing their brand of citizenship for the genre. A nostalgic revival kicked back up in the 2000s, and they could both cash in on that and serve the people who were craving it.

If you caught A Tribe Called Quest during any of this time, you saw a group that looked like it could, potentially, reunite. They weren't playing anything new, but the energy they had was thrilling. During both Rock the Bells tours—but particularly the latter—Tribe was the main attraction. This, on a bill with other heavy-hitting acts from their era: Lauryn Hill, Snoop Dogg, Nas. The crowds would show up in droves for all acts, but most of the excitement was about Tribe. This was layered, of course: Lauryn Hill was erratic and elusive, and Nas and Snoop Dogg were still very much active creators of music. Tribe was the outlier, the greatest novelty act that could be found.

Their shows at Rock the Bells were crowd pleasers, though no one could deny that aesthetically, the group was very different. Phife was heavier, bogged down by his illness and a somewhat stubborn refusal to change his diet and exercise routine with any consistency. Q-Tip would be decked out in a high fade haircut and a leather jacket, despite the summer heat, a completely rebuilt look from his days in Tribe. Phife—remaining customary—would cover himself in an old sports jersey or T-shirt. There was perhaps no better metaphor for the direction of the group's two main vehicles than this one: Phife, clinging to how people saw him then, and Q-Tip, dressing as a version of himself from the future.

Regardless of looks, the group's on-stage synchronicity was as sharp as it ever was. To the naked eye, they were tight, well choreographed, and having a great time. They would rap lines at each other while nodding with approval, finish each other's lines with energy. During one performance on the 2010 Rock the Bells tour, Q-Tip managed to lose his shorts, and he ran through the audience, jumping up and down with the crowd. Their shows in New York were particularly thrilling, with the group bringing out old friends like Busta Rhymes and Consequence to join them on stage to re-create some of their past glory. In a great moment at Rock the Bells New York in 2010, Tribe performed "Bonita Applebum" while the Wu-Tang Clan waited backstage for their time to perform. All members of the group gave in to temptation and began swaying along to the classic they knew, some waving their arms, some clapping on beat.

It was enough to make people forget that the group was apart for a reason. In the early 2010s, rap was even less familiar with the concept of aging than it is now. When rap first started, it was a young man's game, but there was a point in the early 1990s when it seemed like the young men who started it might age into older men who were able to have viable careers well into their aging. But by the time the 2000s came around, that notion was largely shot. Rap had not only become an even younger man's game, but the trends associated with rap had begun switching more and more rapidly. Hip-hop's epicenter, as predicted, moved from New York to Atlanta, and with that came a shifting of sound priorities and a need to always be a step ahead of trends. A Tribe Called Quest was fine existing this way in the nineties, before social media and things like ringtones and streaming. None of these things would have stopped Tribe from having a lot of interest in the realm of new music scenes and communities, but it would have been harder for them to keep up at a pace they wanted to while also making music they deemed meaningful. This is what the real issue was. It wasn't just that older acts were aging out of the genre; it's that it became harder and harder for them to make music that would be both worthwhile to them and commercially impactful enough to sustain their making more music. A Tribe Called Quest was the best novelty act around, but they were still a novelty act, existing with so much enthusiasm, in part, because no one expected or wanted them to get back together and produce anything new.

The documentary seemed like it would be worthwhile because all of the members were still alive and in close enough proximity to one another. It wouldn't be a story told from the depths of the kind of grief that comes after a member of a group has died and the group must put on their best face. Rapaport thought the documentary could be at its most honest by capturing the group in the exact space they were in. Phife, Ali, and Jarobi needed the tours and shows more than Q-Tip did, from a career and financial standpoint. Q-Tip seemed happy to be doing them, but he didn't exactly need to be there. That in and of itself was a tension, one that had existed within the group for almost every iteration of their career: the idea that Q-Tip could be somewhere else, doing something else, but was there to carry the group again.

At the heart of any great music documentary, there has to be either tragedy or conflict. No one really wants to see the story of how a band got to be a band once and how they made a lot of money, lost no friends, and rode off into the sunset unscathed by the music industry. If I tell you that my homies and I weren't homies anymore but had to stick it out for the sake of our shared investment in a thing we'd started, you'd want to know why. If I told you that my homies and I got so close to the promised land we'd imagined that we could rest our palms on the clouds outside the gates, you might understand why we'd want to get there again, despite the fact that it might not be the healthiest endeavor for us.

Beats, Rhymes & Life: The Travels of A Tribe Called Quest is largely about sacrifice, but who is doing the most sacrificing depends on which lens you view the film through. If there is a single thing to be drawn from the film, it is that there is one member who stands in the line of fire in the name of the group. It has long been presented that Q-Tip had to be the person who solely answered for any of A Tribe Called Quest's successes and failures, right or wrong. If there is a person who makes themselves large enough to act as the absorber of all a group's trials, they also get to absorb more than their share of a group's successes.

This was a tipping point for Tribe. Q-Tip took much of the group's heat when things didn't go the way fans thought they should—particularly after *Beats, Rhymes and Life* and *The Love Movement*, when Tribe was just a rap group and no longer an earth-shifting entity. Phife, Jarobi, and Ali Shaheed Muhammad were able to use Q-Tip as a shield from some of that direct criticism: Jarobi because so few people were aware of his role in the group, and Ali because he was so often behind the scenes toiling away. But Phife, whether he wanted to or not, got to use Q-Tip as a shield—the massive personality and creative reputation that Q-Tip brought to the table gave Phife a lot of cushion and comfort in silence. It was Tip who the press wanted to talk to, it was Tip who had to answer for any change in the group's creative direction. It was Phife who showed up and rapped and could pass himself off as going along with the flow.

From another angle, Phife's illness was suffering under the group's rigorous performance, recording, and touring schedule. He was giving himself over to the group's creative whims, particularly during the recording of *Beats, Rhymes and Life*, when he was shuffling back and forth between states. He was one foot out the door, ready to rest and recover with his own life, and then he was back again, thrust into the machinery of a group that he once wasn't even officially a part of. And so, it's all a matter of lens, I suppose.

My group of pals in high school were cooler than I was, by definition. They were good at basketball and I was just okay. They played football, and I watched from the stands. Still, we were cool because, at heart, they were close to what I was: a music nerd who loved ripping CDs from our computers and selling them in our school hallways for $5 a pop, less than what anyone could cop a CD of new music from the store with on release Tuesday. And I was cool enough, sure. But not most popular, by a long shot. Them hanging out with me did more for me than it did for them, at least in terms of reputation and how I could move through the treacherous world of high school. We had our bonds: staying in on Friday nights and eating pizza while talking about rap. Going to sporting events and sharing notes on girls in our class. It was the simplest of things that tethered us, but those echoed the loudest. It didn't matter that their parents had the money to buy them expensive gear and sneakers, and that I had to work to keep up, sometimes sacrificing gas money or lunch.

The things we do to stay close to the people we think will carry us through an entire lifetime . . .

We all decided to go to the same college, right in the city where we knew and loved each other first. In college, something shifted, as things often do. Because I was one of the few black kids at the college, and because of people's fascination with that, I became of significantly more interest than I was in high school. Some of it was desired and much of it not, in retrospect. But at the time, it all felt good, or it all felt worthwhile. It felt like I was finally achieving the popularity I'd watched my friends revel in during our high school years. Now, to hang with me was the prize, and they were reaching for it. Them spending time with me or being seen with me was now more valuable. I would sacrifice plans to spend time with them in their dorm rooms, until I decided not to do that anymore. Until it seemed like too big of a burden for me to bear at this new and big school with seemingly new and endless opportunities for new friendships.

Eventually, we stopped talking altogether. I saw one of them, recently, in a city where neither of us lived, moving through a hotel lobby. We embraced, stiffly. We mentioned something about keeping in touch in a way that didn't seem true.

I think, often, about love strictly as a matter of perspective. For some, it is something they are receiving from someone whom they might slowly be draining the life from.

The Tribe Called Quest documentary is largely about friendship. Yes, it is also about the historical movements of the band, and the group's early days. But mostly, it's about a friendship that is no longer working. Ali and Jarobi are there, of course. But, much like all of A Tribe Called Quest's story, they are secondary to what happens at the center of it. The most painful and fascinating things to watch are the tense moments: a backstage eruption between Q-Tip and Phife, shot on a shaky camera in the dark. The reasons for the tensions are often vague, which would perhaps lead a viewer to imagine that the two don't even know why they're mad at each other anymore, that they've just been mad at each other for so long that it's the only thing they know how to do anymore.

There's something about this that is like love. The way we stay angry at family because we know that, in many cases, they'll be the ones to welcome us back first if we need them to. I fight my dearest homies the loudest and longest because I know they'll pick up my calls when I need them to. Anger is a type of geography. The ways out of it expand the more you love a person. The more forgiveness you might be willing to afford each other opens up new and unexpected roads. And so, for some, staying angry at someone you love is a reasonable option. To stay angry at someone you know will forgive your anger is a type of love, or at least it is a type of familiarity that can feel like love. It might be that Phife and Q-Tip were actually still angry, or it could be that they just needed the comfort of anger to see them through an otherwise difficult and trying reality in which they would otherwise be forced to love each other like they once did, in a past they might not have wanted to return to.

It is also possible that the tension stemmed from more

obvious places: Q-Tip's perfectionism, played out over the band's entire career, and the fact that he was always seen as the group's star despite Phife's immense talent and show-stealing performances. Or the way that some sections of Tribe albums would devolve into showcases for Q-Tip's abilities, long meditations and boasts and production tricks that left Phife on the outside, slightly forgotten. Even when Phife came into his own, it is possible that the group still didn't feel like his.

The central fight in the documentary speaks to this entirely: It was sparked in a moment when Phife, weakened from dialysis treatments, puts an arm around Jarobi to hold him up. Tip attempts to energize the crowd, using Phife as a mascot. "Look alive, y'all!" he yells. "Look at Phife!"

Phife, not amused by his illness being used as a point to hype up the crowd, refuses to speak to Tip backstage, before the physical altercation erupts.

The documentary centers on the two of them, separately and together. When they're apart, doing interviews, largely about each other, the emotional tone is different. Q-Tip is often defiant, telling the camera that he never asked for this, any of it. He never asked to be seen as the Almighty Abstract, and Phife just doesn't understand. He's also relentlessly cool, calm, and adjusted during his interviews, only flashing emotions briefly. Q-Tip, by that point, had been a solo artist in the public eye for so long that he'd almost built up a persona as armor. This doesn't mean that he's not as charming and unique as expected, but his interviews are almost a clinic in self-preservation.

Phife, on the other hand, is open and vulnerable. His grievances are many. He comes close to weeping in several scenes, the ones where he talks about his health, or how unfair it was that he never got what he felt was his due, or the many contentious points he'd hit with Q-Tip. When he speaks of these moments, his voice sometimes trembles, like he is acknowledging for the first time that he and his longtime brother are no longer brothers. Phife's battle with diabetes is highlighted here, making him even more of a sympathetic character. By the time the documentary was being shot, he was full-on in the midst of a search for a kidney donor. The way his illness is handled doesn't feel exploitative, but it still manages to be deeply heartbreaking. Through it all, Phife operates in the documentary like he operated within the group: quick-witted and sharp; confident enough to lie about how confident he truly is; delivering comic lines with ease. In the middle of one rant, Phife goes on and on about refusing to play Tito to Q-Tip's Michael, before taking an aside without skipping a beat and saying "No disrespect to Tito" in a way that is both earnest and hilarious.

The documentary is a measure of how different the two are, and perhaps how different they've always been. Q-Tip, guarded and deeply thoughtful, as if he can see everything he has to lose hanging on the edge of every word bouncing off his tongue. Phife, surprisingly open and eager, like the little brother who finally got enough people wanting to listen to him.

But mostly, it is a documentary about friendship, and about the lengths we go to in order to keep our selfish pride intact, even if it means it's all we have left. Even if the people we love maybe want to see some glimpse of it wash away.

It is comforting to hold on to bitterness, because letting it go means you have nothing but the risk of not being welcomed back into the fold of friendship. In watching the documentary, one realizes that the main character isn't the group itself. The main character is not Q-Tip or Phife, but it is the distance between them and their unwillingness to cross it toward each other, no matter how much a viewer roots for them to do so. They're both stubborn and deeply sensitive in the film—Phife more than Tip at most points—but even in frustration, their friendship is painted so beautifully on screen it is worth rooting for its survival. To hell with the music, let the old friends hug and make up.

In December of 2010, Q-Tip tweeted denouncing the film. "I am not in support of the Tribe Called Quest documentary," he wrote in response to a leaked trailer. As film festivals approached, Q-Tip began calling himself an editor on the film and saying he wanted changes. On a radio show in mid-December 2010, he said:

"I can't really go too much into it but . . . people automatically assume I'm speaking just as the subject, that I'm not supporting it 'cause I ain't like it. I'm a producer on the film, Tribe is a producer on the film. I'm speaking for the whole group . . . Different things need to be done edit-wise. The sentiment of the film is there, 80 percent is there, it's just not done."

Q-Tip, again, was making himself large and speaking for the group at large. He was concerned that the film was being rushed for the festival circuit. When Sundance came, Phife was the only member of Tribe to show up for the film's premiere. The rest sat it out. In March 2011, after the film was acquired by Sony, Q-Tip, Ali, and Jarobi went on MTV and aired out even more issues. They didn't get enough creative control or production credits. They weren't offered the money necessary to travel to Sundance for the film's premiere.

Rapaport was in full defense mode, laying out a business deal that he claimed benefited the Tribe both financially and from a creative control standpoint. He insisted that the group was just emotional about the film and the process that went into making it. He insisted that Tip, Ali, and Jarobi had only seen the movie on a computer screen, and once they saw it on the big screen, they'd be all right with it.

The release was a mess, but the film was still released to critical acclaim. It is difficult to watch, but there's enough roots and "real hip-hop" nostalgia in it to satisfy even the most critical of hip-hop heads. It is a documentary about friendship made by somebody who loves rap. The fact that it was pushed into the world with a high degree of difficulty speaks to the Tribe's legacy. Of course it was never going to be easy.

There is a scene that stands out like no other scene in the film. The most genuine and captivating moment comes in a shot toward the end. Standing to the left of the camera is Q-Tip, and to the right is Phife. By this moment in the film, they've spent most of their time talking about how angry they are at the other one in separate interviews, and speaking tensely to each other in person. The shot takes place in a Manhattan studio while the two are rehearsing for a one-off reunion show. When their music begins playing over the speakers, almost instantly, they break into a completely synchronized dance, as if they are sharing a single body. Q-Tip looks over at Phife, says the words "like this," and Phife follows, right on time. The camera stays on them, and they dance, tethered to each other as if they've never known any other option. As if they were always going to find a way.

CHAPTER TEN

Family Business

MS. CHERYL BOYCE-TAYLOR,

We are maybe each other, through two different mirrors. I know what it is to be a son and long for a living mother. You, a mother, now longing for a living son. When I heard the news, I do admit that I thought first of you. You are not obligated to believe this, of course, but I imagine there are ways in which specific types of loss make kin out of folks who are not kin. I had read the stories about how Malik was born with his kidneys half the size of a normal kidney—begging Him for mercy from the moment you brought him into the world. I had read the stories of how there was an older twin, Mikal, born into the world mere seconds before Malik was born, suffering from the same kidney afflictions. How he held on for eight hours before finally succumbing.

Malik was your only, and I was my mother's youngest. My mother wrote, as you wrote and still write. I like to think that I learned to write first from her, though she didn't teach me English in my earliest youth. It was Arabic that I first learned, writing along the page in a direction I would later fight to unlearn—from the right to the left. I think there is a very particular mercy in being born to a woman who writes, or at least to a woman who sees a world worth writing about.

I am a poet, like you. I came to your work as I came to so much work in the world of poetry: watching, admiring from afar. I first sat on the floor in a crowded New York room in some year when I had traveled to the city maybe listening to your son's raps, as I often did. There was something about the rhythm he held in his voice and the slow crawl of funk layering the instrumentals that made me feel like I was truly in the city. There was always something about the way A Tribe Called Quest negotiated the noise around them, almost becoming it, until everything was awash with a sound you desired.

From the floor of the crowded New York art studio or coffee shop or narrow bar, I could only hear your poems, but not see you. I craned my neck to see early on, but the crowd was drawn so close to you that I accepted my fate, and leaned into the brick that was propping me up. I heard, from murmurs in the back, that you were wearing a Tribe Called Quest T-shirt underneath a slick blazer. Ms. Taylor, I think it might have been better this way, for me to clearly see what you are doing in your work, which I must say is transformational. You are transforming the space.

I love most how you milked the ending of each syllable and let it sing in the air a bit longer. There is a way to read a poem, and then there is a way to allow the poem to exit the body and be read by everyone in the room. The way you, with impeccable rhythm, hung each bit of language from the lights in that room and let me see them, even with my eyes closed. There are beats that happen in between the breaks of words that I think most poets don't tend to understand. There is a way for a reader to manipulate silence so that it is no longer silence but something drawing a listener toward a brief and breathless anticipation that, too, is a type of beat. We know how to read our poems, if nothing else. I say *we* and mean black people, sure. People who have, at some point, clapped on the two and the four. But you, especially, are carrying songs to the people. I found myself, in the back of your reading, humming lowly, as if receiving a spiritual. And I suppose I was, though I didn't know it until now, when reflecting on the moment of that encounter and realizing how healed I was.

I have never been to the town in Trinidad where you come from, Arima. I have read that it is situated between bright red hills. What I love about you is how you fiercely write yourself into your poems and, in doing so, write the reader toward you. I love how richly you integrate Calypso—the social and political aspects of it along with the musical elements of it. I read a part of your poem "A Woman Speaks" out loud to myself often, when trying to figure out how to make language dance with its companions:

Now and then I sit quiet   cup ah coffee in meh hand
listen   hear de words hiss   sing
draw magic in dem breath
rest crimson in de damp gauze of girlhood
dem words weave faded straw into colorful baskets
they hang heart and lungs
teeth and bone

                  meh head almost fall off de side ah meh face
                      an fall fall on meh dauter womb

dem words loop poems 'round moon neck
     and if yuh hear dem hear dem   *write*
   dem down yes we
ah write   ah write   dem down

It's all a song at the end of the day, isn't it? I was at an open mic in the days after Malik passed, and an older black woman came to the microphone and asked everyone to close their eyes. She started into a poem of yours, in respect for your loss. It was such an honor to have you in the room then. The woman was a mother, she said. I imagine she understood a mother's loss, and didn't want your name to be alone or buried. She read "Devouring the Light, 1968"—my favorite of yours. I recited a few lines along:

The day they killed Martin
we could not return to New York City
our visiting senior class stuck in Huntsville
streets blazed with suffering in that small

Alabama town
in the dull shroud of morning
the whole world went crazy
devouring whatever light
that lit our half-cracked windows.

In your son's lyrics, I hear the rhythmic bounce between patois in his flows. The dance between punch line, politics, and boast. I see the Calypso in that, too. Like his verse in Whitey Don's "Artical":

Everytime yuh see mi licked mushitup dancehall
Mc's big or small, mi nuh afraid it dem all
The boyz, dem are jealous cuz see how I'm rock
I try comb voice to represent non'stop
Idiot bwoy, idiot bwoy, idiot bwoy step to side
And in enough room, feature all in my ride

It seems, Ms. Taylor, that we are nothing if not for our histories, and so much of mine is tied up in the business of ghosts. I don't want to burden anyone, but I consider anyone who has lost someone my kin, because I think we are all faced with the same central question of how we go on. How we live the life that best reflects the people who aren't here and are still counting on us.

A mother is never supposed to bury a son, I think. I don't know who makes that rule, as if linear time is the only direction we all have to follow. But something about it seems particularly wrong. A cynic might say that it all depends on the length of life—who had the most fulfilling years and who didn't. But I am not a cynic.

I don't believe much in any natural order. I buried my mother, but at least I was young. I don't remember the day much, but for the dirt that remained on my good pair of dress pants. My family didn't have a lot of money growing up, and I didn't have many reasons to get dressed for nice occasions, and so I only had about one good pair of dress pants. A pair that, I imagine, was passed down from one of my two older brothers. My mother was skilled with sewing—she would sometimes sew together outfits I would wear to school. And so it was nothing to shorten a pair of pants for her youngest child who didn't seem like he would grow past the paltry height he was given already. I cherished the pants, I think, because being young and poor, I maybe clung to what I was told was a nice thing.

I didn't dig much of the grave—maybe none, if I recall. I do recall kicking the dirt around it, though. It seemed so odd to me at the time, to have a living person to hold a mere three days earlier, now having dirt heaved atop their body. Sometime during the kicking I got a dark stain of wet dirt on my pants. I remember staring at it on the ride home, and then while sitting on my bed after the funeral. I remember thinking that I had betrayed the fabric, this item that my mother had worked so hard on for me to wear and feel nice, or briefly wealthy. Focusing on the stain and mourning the pants, I think, allowed me to mourn the greater loss. I was mourning something that my mother had poured her heart into for me, because I was her son. And so, this is how I remember mourning my mother: by way of soiling something that she crafted for me with her bare hands. The stain came out after two washes, though I often wished it hadn't.

I am wondering what, if anything, you held in your hands after Malik died. What you still might hold in your hands today. I know it is different to lose a person who was distinctly yours but also everyone's. What is that feeling? Is it better or worse? To have a loss be something you are mourning in a singular way, which is not the way everyone else is mourning, though perhaps they think it is. On the day I heard the news, I first sat down on my couch and then instinctively checked every corner of the internet I could, hoping it wasn't true. Death is such a reckless and unexpected visitor, waiting to make a mess of our past, present, and future in equal measures.

I am not here asking for a reliving of the moment, but I am here, instead, to say thank you for raising a writer. I was raised by a woman who wrote, and I don't know if that means anything other than the fact that I saw language as a way to get free at an early age. She wrote a book that she didn't live long enough to finish. I have all of the books you've written, stacked outside of my bookcase, which has long since run out of room. I am saying that I love words, and I have long appreciated what you do with them. And all of this time I was listening to Malik rap, I was hearing your fingerprints. You raised a literary figure—someone who knew his way around verse and punch line and clever turn of phrase. At the heart of his writing and yours was the same driving force: themes of the vast black interior—hair texture, and skin color, inner and outer strife, and the small joys that must be unlocked to survive it all.

I knew I would miss him when he was gone. I always did. But I thank you, particularly, for still living and writing. For the way you let the syllables dance around each other in the air when you read your poems. The way you let words hang above an audience and linger way up with the dimming lights in a room, until they fade and fade, and eventually fall away for good, a fresh memory.

TIP,

I once closed my fist and swung it across my older brother's cheek. It was something my sister, older than both of us, demanded I do. I had to be about eleven, or maybe twelve. I don't think I knew what I was doing. It is one thing to witness violence but another entirely to understand it for yourself by the swelling of pain that comes when your hand collides with someone else's bones. Despite being only about a year older than I was, my brother was bigger and undoubtedly stronger than I was. He wasn't necessarily a bully so much as I was constantly an annoyance. And yet, I found myself often on the losing end of fights. The logic, my sister said, was to assert some type of power over the larger, more dominant sibling in the room. And so, during a game of cards, I crashed a closed fist into my brother's cheek and then ran and hid in a closet until he calmed down.

This didn't change our relationship in any great measure, but it did grant me a brief bit of thrill. I know that feeling, and the desire to chase it. When you are the little brother, even if you are only younger by a handful of months, or only little by way of stature, you do what you must not to be entirely overshadowed.

My brother is still living, so I do not yet regret the times I was less than good to him. I will, and I know I will, but there isn't any road to that for me yet. It might happen over years. We'll both go gray in our beards and begin to lose the things that marked us as young. I can prepare, in due time, my long list of apologies for those things I cannot carry with me after he's gone. There will be a discussion of the weight to these things—the things we keep inside ourselves when we lose someone close to us with whom we used to share a knowledge and history.

Or it might happen suddenly, as it did for you. Someone there in the night and gone in the morning before all can be resolved. When just enough has been resolved to work as you did once before, as brothers do.

In the years when you and Phife were not speaking, I looked at the old *Source* magazine cover from time to time. I hung it on my walls—first in a bedroom and then in a dorm room, and then, briefly, on the wall of an ill-fated apartment. It was a reminder of a very specific kind of heartbreak. You all were like family to me. So much like my brother and me. You, the one who seemed infallible—skilled at all things. Phife, the exciting but sometimes under-the-radar sidekick.

What I always loved about you both was the fact that you needed each other, regardless of whatever else came along. Yes, I did love the solo albums, Tip. There was no question they were going to be great. Your brand as a musician is that of someone who is too talented and too curious to be anything other than great when left to your own devices. And I know you were trying all things except to capture the magic of Tribe, but I will admit that I found a spark missing. You and Phife needed each other in the same way that Mick and Keith did or Simon and Garfunkel did. It is one thing to make magic, and another to make miracles. The magic can be conjured by anyone skilled enough to pull off a prolonged trick. But a miracle is something that seems as though it will never be seen again, no matter how skilled the people making it are. Phife allowed you the possibility for miracles. And I know. I know it was hard: to keep him focused and on task; to drag him off the streets or the subways. I know that all of these things take a toll, begin to feel as if you are holding up an entire group on your own while wondering what your individual ambitions might get you.

I know a bit about resentment, for I have been both the fist swinging at the cheek of someone I resented and the stinging cheek that cradled a jealous fist. I don't know if Phife wanted to be like you so much as he wanted space to be himself. And no matter what else your relationship yielded, I'm glad that you afforded him that space, even when it seemed as if you weren't. I can't imagine how hard it must have been, to both fight for yourself and fight for your brother, when your brother didn't seem to be fighting for himself.

It isn't like the *Low End* days, Tip. The police killed Rodney King on a grainy video then. The camera shook, and one might have to look closely to see the body twitching on the ground. From afar, it looked as if the black batons were crashing into a single black mass. Now, there is death on video everywhere.

Clear shots of it. From body or dashboard cams, or from cell phone videos shot on sidewalks. We are perhaps at the true low end now: the place where sound only exists to rattle this freshly tiled killing floor. There are more than enough things that I can't let go of these days—my fear, my rage, my sadness. I haven't got as much room for guilt as I used to, despite how it haunts and wishes to crawl out of me at each opening of my mouth around anyone I have once not loved as I should have.

There's a thing with siblings that so many people without them don't understand. How you can punch each other until the skin pulled over your ribs begins to bruise, and how that violence is also done out of a type of love. When I watched you and Phife on the documentary, I noticed it all right away. All you ever wanted was for him to survive, for him to get right. But you know how it is. We're all the youngest somewhere, in some room. We're all going to be the quiet, forgotten one who does the largest thing possible to stand out. You said it yourself, moments after he was gone, when I logged onto Twitter, looking for a sign that this all might be a joke, one more prank played by Malik. But there was your tweet:

He left me with the gift of unconditional love and brotherhood that will NEVER be lost with me . . . Ever

May we love our brothers, Tip. May we love them after they are gone, sure. But may we love them even when they fill us with rage, or even when we don't speak to them for years, or even when we close our fists and our eyes and swing in their direction with all we have.

MALIK,

I am mad on behalf of your leaving, largely because the Knicks never got it together for you. This is maybe not the time or place, as I am conversing with the you that is no longer here in the physical sense. But I wanted, more than anything, for the Knicks to provide you with some small relief before it was all said and done. The "it," of course, is the "it" of your living, which came to an end before I expected. Before any of us did. Still, it was the run of empty years that most left me sad for you. The Melo years. In the photos of you late in your career, I remember you in the Knicks gear most: in the old NYK shirt on stage at Rock the Bells with Tip, or slouching in an interview with an oversized Oakley jersey. I wanted them to make it out of the first round of the playoffs at least. But maybe it all makes sense, doesn't it? To root for what some might see as the lovable losers, stumbling over themselves on the way to near-misses and outright disasters. If one has no hopes at all, even the smallest bit of joy can be a relief.

It has been raining all day, and I am thinking about the water, Malik. I am thinking of the mixture of water and sugar, which is to say I am thinking about Kool-Aid. They will talk of what killed you and what has killed many black people before you as something simple. Sugar, a vice that one might consider easy to let go if a doctor says your life depends on letting it go. When you grew up in a family like mine—not the poorest family on the block but certainly not rich—Kool-Aid was a staple. The ingredients were accessible: all you needed was sugar and water. The actual drink was inexpensive in the time of my childhood. The small packs of powder made half a gallon of the drink, and only sold for a dime, ten for a dollar. In my house, when we went shopping every other Friday on payday, everyone got their own pick of Kool-Aid packets. My brother and I would get a handful each, him tropical punch and me black cherry. They were supposed to last us for the two weeks in between shopping trips, and often didn't. The true test in my neighborhood, and in my household, was how sweet your Kool-Aid was. Unlike other drinks that one might purchase premade and already packaged in a container, Kool-Aid was at the mercy of the preparer's hands. Kool-Aid instructions call for one cup of sugar per packet, but specifies "more or less to taste." A friend's mother once joked about that specific instruction. She threw her head back and laughed in her kitchen and said that Kool-Aid put that there for black folks, while she blindly poured another scoop of sugar into the dark red water while she stirred.

I became attached to the taste, or the feeling, or being able to dictate my own sweetness with my own money. The summer *Beats, Rhymes and Life* came out, I biked long and hard through the streets of my neighborhood with headphones on and a CD player in my pocket, your verse in "The Hop" dancing off my tongue with the taste of dark red sugar water, the part where you rhyme *"Word is bond I am the baddest / And all you honies out there, word is bond, you know my status."* Over winter break in 1993, I sat in the back of a car driven by my oldest brother, stomach weighed down with sugar from candy, while *Midnight Marauders* bled from the speakers, and I dipped back into my packet of Fun Dip, a candy that was literally colored sugar that was eaten with a makeshift spoon that was also pretty much sugar, while you rapped *"My man Al B. Sure, he's in effect mode / Used to have a crush on Dawn from En Vogue / It's not like honey dip would wanna get with me"* in "Oh My God." When *The Love Movement* came out in the fall of 1998, I sat in headphones on the back of a school bus, eating one of the Little Debbie snacks that you could still get out of the school vending machine for just fifty cents while listening to "Busta's Lament," where you rapped *"So what's the deal Captain / if it's time for some action / Watch me roll with hon, try to push her back."*

And on the day I read of your death, I had my hand in a bowl of candy that I had purchased a few days earlier from a shop in Mystic, Connecticut, where I went specifically for the candy, on the way to Providence, Rhode Island. I went because I knew they had the candy I loved, and I was driven to spend my own money to dictate my own sweetness once again. And when I saw the news of your dying, I was biting into a cherry sour and letting the sugar coat my teeth, and I was reaching for more, and they will say that you died because you loved sugar too much to stop letting it kill you, but some things we cling to because we come from people who clung to them.

And, Malik, I hope black children are still riding bikes with the taste of Kool-Aid dancing off their tongues. Today, on the day you are gone, I hope every bodega and every corner store gave away Kool-Aid by the cup. I hope kids went to stores with their parents' money and walked out with pocketfuls of candy. I want candy thrown from the cliffs. I want candy to rattle off of my roof now instead of the water from the sky while your verses play. I want my people to take better care of themselves, but I wanted a day for us to revel in what you loved, if only for a moment. I read about how much soda you drank, how much fried and sweet food you popped even when the clock hung over your head, and I want better health for us all. But let us put our sugar down tomorrow. Let us return to our doctors and receive the bad news of our undoing some other time. Let us go to the gym, but not on this day. I wish people would have drowned the streets in sugar before dancing in them. I wish people would have put sugar on that which was already sweet. I wish every verse of yours I could remember mentioned honey or something else sweet. Today there is a sweetness on my tongue that feels as though it may never leave.

I do not wish you to be reduced to a cautionary tale in the moments after your death. I know it will happen. Already, there are people on the internet, reminding black men to get their health together and all of that. I understand. But to me, you were a titan first. A literary figure of the highest order, who drew a bridge between popular culture and lyrical wizardry with a type of belligerence and fearlessness. You, inventor of the smooth punch line, not like the ones tumbling clumsily out of pens and speakers now. You did punch-line rap the way it should have been done: less like a witty pun, more like a matter-of-fact statement; something you truly believed, not something you were using to score points. I always wanted to be the only one in the room to get the last line of your bars. It always felt like unlocking a puzzle.

I know *The Love Movement* was not easy. It is a belabored album, and it sounds every bit of it. But I love it more than I love anything else, Malik. I could hear you and Tip looking for exits in every track—the sound of a group that maybe made one album too many but still had some magic left. But I love it because of how brightly your star shined while trying to fight off the inevitable morning. On "His Name Is Mutty Ranks," there you were. Alone, for two minutes, doing what you did.

"For God so loved the world he said Phife, ask your preacher / Love to toot my own Horne, similar to Lena."

Those two minutes are how I will remember you, Malik, today and always. I wanted so much more for you after the Tribe's split. I wanted you to be adored, appreciated beyond belief. I wanted you to release iconic solo albums, sell out shows, and make it to the top of the mountain again. Alone this time, so there could be no debate about your greatness.

In the days after you were buried, I heard that you and Tip had been working on an album. The Tribe had been planning a comeback for a year. You were going to surprise us all. But there you were, dying too soon, and shaking the surprise out early. Always making the group bend to your singular pace.

It seemed, in the gloom of an already-long year, that this is how fairy tales end. This is the way to make yourself endless, after already making yourself immortal. It is still spring, and the album won't be here until fall. A whole world seems eager and excited to unfold in front of us between now and then. It seemed we'd get to hear your living voice one last time, before it was lost to nostalgia forever.

Malik, I am sorry that we did not gather roses for you when you could still clutch the petals in your hands and feel the softness of them stick with you for ages, the way so many of your verses stuck to our tongues with the sweetness we allowed ourselves sometimes, days after we first heard them. Malik, Phife Dawg, Five Foot Assassin, you towered over an era of incredible riches. You, creator of another narrative. Patron saint of the punch line. You, who got the party started and stuck around long enough to get the last laugh. Malik, we will remember you when a rapper tries to be clever and fails; when a crowd cheers at a half-hearted rhyme. We will suck our teeth at club DJs, and take the long way home. We will press play on anything that bears your name, and let you fill a room, or a car, or the space on an empty train. We will remember how you did it once with so much ease. On point. All the time, on point.

CHAPTER ELEVEN

Common Ground

The fact that Leonard Cohen was dead didn't help matters. He fell in his home on November 7, 2016, and then died in his sleep. No one knew that he was dead for three days. His family didn't alert the world until the tenth, when the world had already shifted into a place that felt darker. *Darkness* is what Leonard Cohen asked of our preferences in the title of his final album, *You Want It Darker*, which was released mere weeks before his fall. It was the kind of album you make when you know you're going to die. The song "Leaving the Table" opens with the lines "I'm leaving the table / I'm out of the game," and to a close listener, they might say that is when they knew that "the game" was the Big Game, the one we're all playing until we aren't anymore.

Leonard Cohen recorded *You Want It Darker* in the living

room of his home, because he could barely move anymore. After a rigorous tour schedule in the late 2000s and early 2010s, he started to suffer from spine fractures. There is some mercy, I imagine, in living a life long enough to know when death is coming for you. To be obsessed with mortality at age eighty-two reads a lot more romantically than it does in your late twenties, which is how old Cohen was when he met Marianne Ihlen in Greece, shortly after Ihlen had returned to her native Norway to find out that her husband had abandoned her. I take issue with the word "muse" when it is attached to a woman who is written about extensively by a man—as if she serves no other purpose. Ihlen and Cohen built a small life together, at least as much of a life as one can from afar, through various infidelities and across oceans. When Cohen traded writing poems for recording songs, a photo of Marianne appeared on the back cover of his second album, *Songs from a Room*. In the photo, Marianne is sitting at a desk in a bedroom, fingers on a typewriter, wearing only a towel.

As his career as a singer-songwriter took off, Cohen's relationship with Marianne started to dissolve. Cohen wrote songs about her: "Bird on the Wire," "Hey, That's No Way to Say Goodbye," and "So Long, Marianne," the latter a slow pour of heartbreak that stretches out long and dark. This is how someone becomes known only by what their love has inspired in the heart of someone else, I suppose. Cohen and Marianne stayed in touch, writing letters and visiting each other when possible.

In July of 2016, Cohen got an email from a close friend of Marianne's informing him that Marianne wasn't well. It was cancer, he was told. Marianne had been diagnosed earlier that month. When she and Cohen spoke then, she didn't tell him that she was sick, near death. She was eighty-one then, and her relationship with Cohen had spanned over five decades. She only had a few days of life left, so Cohen stopped working on his album about death and mercy and wrote her back immediately. He wrote:

> Well Marianne, it's come to this time when we are really so old and our bodies are falling apart and I think I will follow you very soon. Know that I am so close behind you that if you stretch out your hand, I think you can reach mine. And you know that I've always loved you for your beauty and your wisdom, but I don't need to say anything more about that because you know all about that. But now, I just want to wish you a very good journey. Goodbye old friend. Endless love, see you down the road.

Two days later, Marianne would be dead, dying in her sleep. But not before she was read Cohen's letter out loud, and not before she could laugh and lift a hand when the part was read about how close he was behind her.

And, of course, he was. Like Marianne, Cohen would go in the dark calm of sleep. I know not what the final moments before death are like, but I hardly imagine they are always worth being awake for. Particularly if you've lived as long a life as Cohen, as Marianne. They both went calmly, after some ill had befallen them. If there is no way to make living forever appealing, let me say that I hope to live a full life loudly, and then slink off into death quietly, perhaps holding the also-sleeping hand of someone I have loved for so long that their emotional architecture has grown into mine.

I thought about Marianne first when I heard the news of Cohen. Specifically, I thought about what it is like to be tethered to someone or something for so long that their exit rolls out the red carpet for your own. It's like if you love someone or something or someplace for long enough, they or it become embedded in your heart. And so their death becomes a small death of your own. Leonard Cohen loved a person enough to grow old as she grew old, and then loved her enough to want to follow her to what might be a better place.

I'd seen this happen enough—like with June Carter Cash and Johnny Cash—that I spent the months after Phife died wondering who loved him enough to go with him. If it would be Q-Tip, who hitched his star to Phife's for so long that surely his passing left an immeasurable void. If it would be one of the other members of Tribe, or perhaps Phife's mother, who spent a lifetime writing poems as gentle and generous as Cohen's once were. But death didn't echo into anyone else's chamber, perhaps because everyone was still too young. Everyone had hearts still strong enough to survive whatever years came next. Perhaps because they all still had work to do, and Leonard Cohen had done his already. Leonard Cohen went to sleep on November 7, 2016, and never woke up to the darkness he was asking for.

I watched the country turn red on a television screen while sitting on a couch, and I imagine the historians years from now will try to convince the world that everyone knew this was coming. The US presidential election cycle always feels long, but this one—most prominently featuring Donald Trump and Hillary Clinton—felt exceptionally draining. It didn't help that the year itself was mired in seemingly endless tragedies, particularly a summer that opened with a terrorist attack at Pulse nightclub in Orlando, which killed forty-nine people and wounded over fifty others. In July, on back-to-back days, police officers murdered two unarmed black men: Alton Sterling in Baton Rouge, Louisiana, and Philando Castile in Falcon Heights, Minnesota. Philando Castile was murdered while reaching for a permit to show that he was allowed to carry the weapon he informed an officer that he had in his car. The officer shot Castile in the torso several times. His girlfriend, Diamond Reynolds, live-streamed his death on Facebook. It was a jarring scene, Castile bleeding to death in his car's driver's seat while Reynolds asked the officer why he shot Castile in the first place. In all of the videos of black people dying that had begun to more prominently circle the internet, none of them had ever been broadcasted in real time. It is one thing to watch the life slip away from someone as they age, expecting them to go. But to watch death snatch a person while scrolling through a news feed littered with pictures of dogs or posts about vacation plans seemed too surreal. It felt as if the portrait of death could arrive at any time and turn your face to it right when you'd forgotten it.

Castile's case got more attention, in part because of the unique nature of the filming and the general idea that his

killing seemed very blatantly unjust—though the police officer, Jeronimo Yanez, was acquitted in June of 2017. I found myself more fascinated by Alton Sterling, who sold CDs. Sterling
was what most neighborhoods would call "the CD Man," and
any neighborhood I spent my youth and adolescence in had
one. Every high school in the Columbus Public Schools system
had one. When I worked at the mall in my late teens and early
twenties at a shoe store called Underground Station, the CD
Man was named Tony and he'd come in every Thursday, because he knew that's when the direct deposit hit for everyone
in the mall. The CD Man sometimes has DVDs and sometimes
has electronics and sometimes has free advice. The CDs and
DVDs aren't like the ones you can buy in stores—they're
burned copies, sometimes with cheaply printed-out album
art on the cover. But for that, you get a deal: sometimes one
CD is $7, but you could get two for $10, or three for $15. It was a
blessing for those of us who were young and trying to hold on
to what money we had, working jobs selling shoes or coffee or
books in a mall for $8 an hour.

Tony took requests, which was all I ever hit him for. I had
my own CD-burning software at home, but it was often a
hassle to get old discs from the library and burn them. I once
requested that Tony bring me all of A Tribe Called Quest's dis-
cography, because, at that point, I still only had them on cassette and this was the early 2000s, when cassettes were relics,
and CDs weren't far behind but still had currency in my car,
with its custom-installed CD player that cost more than the
car itself. He returned the next week with every Tribe album,

in chronological order, with printed-out album art for each one and a handwritten tracklist on the back. He charged me $20 for the whole lot.

After I left my job at the mall, I'd see Tony from time to time on the block, selling CDs out of a plastic bag. We'd always say what's up, and I'd ask him how business was going, and he'd tell me "slow, but I'm doing all right." Until I stopped seeing him altogether around 2007 or so. I later heard that he'd gotten busted selling crack outside of where the old mall used to be. He'd gotten linked up with someone from out of town and was pushing all of their work for them. He got sentenced to ten years, I was told. CDs became less of a needed entity, and hustlers adapt to their environment.

Alton Sterling, though, just had CDs and DVDs. He sold them outside of the Triple S Food Mart. He was a neighborhood fixture, sitting outside the market with a table from the afternoon until the early morning, playing music and selling CDs and DVDs to people passing by. He kept his business going by being tuned in to the community and its needs, despite the fact that CDs, by 2016, were not the preferred medium for music listening, and DVD players were all but a thing of the past, relegated to the graveyard by streaming services. If someone wanted classical music or a DVD of a film from the 1960s, Sterling would track it down, sometimes within twenty-four hours. The neighborhood he sold in was dangerous, and worried his loved ones, in whose name he hustled. What people might not understand is that there is no mercy like the mercy that comes with being beloved in a violent place. If you are vital to the fabric of even the most violent place, that place will keep you alive for as long as it can, and Sterling was vital to the Triple S Food Mart and the people around it.

But he still carried a gun, because stories began floating around about other CD vendors being robbed in the area. And so when police were called to the Triple S Food Mart in response to a man threatening someone with a firearm, there was Alton Sterling.

Sure, after Sterling's death, the store owner specified that it wasn't Sterling who drove him to call the police. But when they arrived, he was there. Alton Sterling was large, both hard to miss and hard to control. I think often of how someone large and black is seen as a vessel for love or a vessel for fear, depending on who is doing the looking. When Sterling was tased and wrestled to the ground by police, his gun fell out of his waistband.

I don't need to tell you how many bullets followed, or that the officers eventually walked free, or that the Triple S market no longer has a CD Man, or that Alton Sterling didn't get to go home to the people who worried that a neighborhood would kill him instead of a country. Whenever there is a black person murdered at the hands of police and then also a video of it, there is a lot to process: anger, fear, resentment, anxiety. But with Sterling, I was also processing what happens when music is ripped from a community in that fashion; when the person you rely on for a soundtrack bleeds out on a street at thirty-seven years old, long before age might take them in a more peaceful fashion.

The map of the United States turned red on my television on November 8, 2016, and Leonard Cohen was dead but no one knew that yet, and Alton Sterling and Philando Castile were dead, and more mass shootings were happening seemingly every week, and I guess this is what a country can get away with when people consider themselves afraid. Donald Trump won the presidency. In coming hours and days and months, I will tell people that I knew it was going to happen, which is only half true. There is knowing, and then there is hoping against that knowing. Halfway through the election coverage—which I told myself I wasn't going to watch in the first place— I decided, on a whim, to take a nap. Things were seemingly starting to break bad for Hillary Clinton, and I imagined that maybe if I fell asleep, I'd wake up in a better or newer country. When I did wake up, it was around two in the morning, and I stumbled into my living room to look at my phone, inundated with messages of anger, despair, and grief from friends, some of whom I hadn't talked to in years. Most of them black, sending some generic but needed message of solidarity, drenched in a backdrop of fear. I didn't turn on the television.

I stayed in bed the next morning. No one I knew had heard any of the Tribe Called Quest album that was promising to be released in just two days, on Friday, November 11. The group hadn't released any singles ahead of the album, and outside of a press run after Phife's death announcing the album, they had been pretty silent about it altogether. I called in favors, I asked even the most reliable sources I knew, and no one had heard the album. On Thursday, I had to drive to Philadelphia to prepare to read poems in a room of people. Thursday morning, I'd heard Leonard Cohen was dead. I didn't know he'd been dead for days. I thought it was the election that did him in.

We Got It from Here . . . Thank You 4 Your Service was released a few moments before midnight on Thursday, November 10, 2016. In Philadelphia, everyone wanted to talk about politics. In the grocery stores, at the gas stations, in line at Popeyes. Pennsylvania went red, much to the dismay of Philly, a decidedly blue area. It is hard to describe the tone of the country now, looking back. All I remember is seeing some of the country triumphant and an entirely other half of the country dejected, wondering how they would live through it all. The calls for resistance and organizing came a few months later, but in the immediate aftermath, there was a haze over everything, one that I imagine will be difficult to explain to people who weren't living in it. I casually asked folks on the street how they were and got long, honest answers.

I read poems that Thursday night in a small room packed to the walls. People were sitting on the floor and on top of the bar. The organizers of the reading told me that the crowd usually wasn't as big as it was, but they imagined that people needed to hear poetry that night. Some, sad about Cohen; all, sad about our country's new predicament, which was our country's old predicament, or our country's forever predicament. At the end of the night, unsure what else to do, I found a Leonard Cohen poem on my phone. One I liked and remembered well. The poem "Do Not Forget Old Friends" is short, a poem about bidding an inevitable farewell, and it maybe fit the mood, but maybe didn't.

> *Do not forget old friends*
> *you knew long before I met you*
> *the times I know nothing about*
> *being someone*
> *who lives by himself*
> *and only visits you on a raid.*

"The Space Program" is the song that opens *We Got It from Here*, and it opens with a sample from the 1974 blaxploitation film *Willie Dynamite*.

> *I'mma deal with a bigger insult, man*
> *The heat, the heat, the heat, the heat*
> *It's comin' down hard*
> *We've got to get our shit together*

The scene is from Willie—pimp and title character—at a meeting where he is attempting to organize the other pimps against the police presence cracking down on them, rather than fighting among themselves for turf that was equally threatened by all of the same issues. But that's not where the album starts. One might think the album starts with Q-Tip and Phife Dawg's voices coming into harmony right after the sampled monologue, rapping "Gotta get it together / gotta get it together for sisters / for mothers and fathers and dead niggas," but the album doesn't start there, either.

At the opening of verse one. Q-Tip, his voice unraveled from his dead brother's, raps:

Word to Phifer / Gonna bring it to the overlord . . .

That's when the album starts.

During my first year in college, a kid on my dorm floor kept a small tape recorder next to his bed. On it was a recording of his grandmother, simply talking. It was unspectacular to everyone but him, of course. College freshmen did things like this in the days before FaceTime or Skype, when you often had to share a phone with three other people in a single room, and privacy was rare. The reality, though, was that his grandmother was gone and this was all he had left. She had died the spring before, so he held on to her voice, speaking of the mundane. I think about this often, perhaps always. By that I mean that I am always thinking about how we keep our ghosts close to us—how we store them and pull them out of our closets when we most need their memories—how, if we're lucky, we have a new echo to mix in with the old.

My favorite story about Q-Tip is the one where, in 1991, when A Tribe Called Quest were coming off of their stunning and critically acclaimed debut album, *People's Instinctive Travels and the Paths of Rhythm*, an interviewer asked him if he was afraid of a sophomore jinx. Q-Tip scoffed, "'Sophomore jinx'? What the fuck is that? I'm going to make *The Low End Theory*." This is the best Q-Tip story, the one that has defined the most formative aspect of his sprawling vision: an eye toward the work, without ever glancing over his shoulder. Even if it is never explicitly spoken, most musical groups, across genres, are sold to us with a single genius in the center; everyone else in the group just adds to the canvas after the visionary has his or her turn at it. This person is also the group's propeller, pushing them past whatever boundaries they thought they'd hit. The Beach Boys had Brian Wilson. TLC had Left Eye. A Tribe Called Quest has had Q-Tip. They've always had Q-Tip, even when it seemed impossible for him to keep going.

It's the Saturday night after the album's release, and on the television, Q-Tip's shoulders look as heavy as I've ever seen them. Over his left shoulder on the *Saturday Night Live* stage is the face of Phife Dawg, Malik, his dearly departed brother, cocreator, sometimes rival. He is at the tail end of "The Space Program," shouting into his microphone: "Let's make something happen, let's make something happen, let's make something happen!" When the song finally winds down, Q-Tip turns to walk off the stage and is embraced by Busta Rhymes—the kind of hug that someone gives to another person they have walked through battle with. Jarobi joins the hug, and then Consequence, while Phife looks down on them, both literally and in any spiritual way that one could hope for.

There they are, after a hellish week, the almighty Tribe Called Quest, not through with us yet. Q-Tip's shoulders fall and his left arm, even in the embrace, goes slack, like it is anticipating having to hold someone else.

The fascinating thing about *We Got It from Here . . . Thank You 4 Your Service*, is how it sat, sonically, within the 2016 hip-hop landscape. Sure, perhaps the answer is that A Tribe Called Quest were always ahead of their time, making music that sounded futuristic yet still touchable. But even considering that, it was stunning to hear how much of the album felt like a slightly updated version of the same brilliant sound that A Tribe Called Quest crafted in the 1990s—a fresh download of everything, but newer and cleaner. They didn't sound bitter about the genre, or jaded about its evolution. They are architects, after all—builders who don't bow to the land but know how to make the land bow to them. It was still percussion- and jazz-leaning intricacies. It was still the occasional surprising guitar or horn, coming out of nowhere to glue a song together. And, yes, it was still Q-Tip's breathless, run-on sentence flow, the words bleeding into each other until the language itself becomes an instrument. And, yes, there was Phife here, too. Maybe it's just how much I needed them to still be young, but I don't think anyone sounded older. Phife, still on his toes, shit-talking and praising in the same breath: "You clowns be bum sauce / Speak my name, it's curtains / Hamdulillah, my crew's back to workin'," and you can tell he means it.

The verses of the dead are a funny thing. I want, more than anything, to put a seashell to my ear and hear not the ocean but the voices of everyone I once loved who are now gone. Listening to Phife's brilliance on this album was both stunning and heartbreaking in that way—you press stop on a voice and the voice is truly stopped, but sometimes it's not. Also, because of his minimal solo output over the years, and because history sometimes paints him only as Q-Tip's sideman, it was easy to forget the things Phife did so well in his prime. He's still as punchy and clever as he always was, delightfully tongue-in-cheek ("Fourth grade reading level but he knows how to rap" on "Whateva Will Be") and still drops the occasional up-to-date sports reference ("Status, Chris Paul and John Wall in the league" on "Dis Generation"). It's a late reminder of what drew so many of us to Phife in the first place. A reminder that is more potent now, of course, but one that echoes long after the music ends.

It's impossible to speak of this album without also speaking of the time it arrived in. The second song, "We the People . . ." is powered by its mocking, scathing hook: "All you Black folks, you must go / All you Mexicans, you must go / And all you poor folks, you must go / Muslims and gays / Boy, we hate your ways / So all you bad folks, you must go . . ." It's the voice of America turned in on itself, the voice that many of us pretended was at a distance until it was a consistent and low drone, until it had begun activating the most violent among us, from the highest office in the country. It's jarring, to hear a sentiment made that plain in a week when the country vomited on its own shirt and then looked around and asked who made the mess. It says what we've known all along, even as people now wring their hands, eager for the "new" art that marginalized people will create: Black folks have been creating with their backs against the wall for years, telling the future, speaking what is coming to the masses that aren't eager to hear it until what's coming actually arrives, looming over them.

It struck me, in the moment, that critically dissecting an album felt even smaller than it usually does. The times are urgent, and I know nothing but going back to what I love, but music still feels tiny and disposable. I think, though, that perhaps we will cling to our art and learn to truly love our artists. I am not OK, and even if I were to find the time to be OK, there are too many people I love who are not OK, and I feel that weight on top of my own. And yet, with the world still crumbling under its various political ills, and everyone covered in our respective heaviness, A Tribe Called Quest rose again, and they were also not OK. You can hear it in the album's gentler moments, the songs where Q-Tip is largely alone, like the somber and sparse "Melatonin," where he opens his first verse: "The understudy for the star / The show must go on."

The show, it seems, ends here, and we didn't even deserve for it to take us this far. Earlier that year, I didn't think I wanted another Tribe Called Quest album. Then Phife died, and I wanted another Tribe Called Quest album more than anything. Then it arrived, and it was even greater than I could ever have asked for. The heroic and brilliant Tribe Called Quest, who almost certainly have nothing left to give us now; the greatest rap group of all time, who returned in a week when the world caught fire to give us one final everlasting gift. It's one way to keep a beloved ghost in our ears, no matter what uncertain hell awaits.

There is another story about Leonard Cohen that I think about all the time. Toward the end of the seventies, when Cohen's popularity was waning, he retreated to Hollywood to record the album *Death of a Ladies' Man*. The album was produced by Phil Spector, who, by that point, had spiraled into a whirlwind of erratic and violent behavior, carrying guns, pointing and shooting them at random. During the recording of John Lennon's 1975 album *Rock 'N' Roll*, Spector fired off a pistol in the studio. His production had also suffered since his 1960s heyday, making Cohen and Spector kind of in need of each other, in hopes for a big hit.

When the album was released, the response was predictably lukewarm. Drowned in Spector's bag of tricks, the album hardly had much of the traditional Cohen in it that audiences were looking for. The story I think about, though, comes from the recording session. In the depths of them, during the recording of the nine-minute title track—which took an entire day—Spector, at random, put a loaded pistol to the neck of Cohen and cocked the gun. "I love you, Leonard," he said. Cohen, without blinking or without panic, calmly responded "I hope you love me, Phil." Spector lowered the gun.

All of this is about mercy. I'm talking about what it is to be from a place that promises to love you while holding a gun to your neck. I'm talking about what it feels like to have the gun lowered, briefly, by the hands of some unseen grace. Sometimes, it is a protest that stretches long into a night, or sometimes it is a reading where a room hears familiar words and cries along with you as you read them out loud. But sometimes, it is a perfect album that arrives just in time to build a small community around you. To briefly hold a hand over your eyes and make a new and welcoming darkness of the world outside, even when it is on fire.

CHAPTER TWELVE

**Thank You
4 Your Service**

The Grammy Awards aren't supposed to be political. They pretend to be, in the ways that all award shows pretend to be: artists take to the stage during their acceptance speeches and sometimes present a half-hearted rallying cry for or against something in the political moment. The Grammy Awards, in particular, cater to this type of performance, as its audience is one that likes to pretend that music is still an untouched political force. The result at the Grammys is a special type of clumsy, though. Artists get on stage and stumble through half-thought-out opinions on issues that they perhaps haven't had the time to fully dive into. The performers who are especially passionate and well researched often go on too long, getting awkwardly played off by a chorus of strings. Few performers actually use their performance space to make a statement, even though it is the one time when they are on stage with the entire audience looking at them and at least have a more flexible time range to make a point. It all makes for a messy bit of performative politics—the kind that sends fans running to the internet and asking why their beloved musicians don't simply stick to music.

Despite this, the Grammy Awards also have a relationship with rap music that is tenuous, at best. Even though it has spent the most recent decade attempting to make up for it with its nominations and by affording more stage space to rappers, it cannot be ignored that on its face, it seems as if the Grammys think about rap as a lesser genre. Since 1989, when rap was first introduced to the Grammys as a category, only two rap albums have won Album of the Year. It bears mentioning that the two albums—Outkast's *Speakerboxxx / The Love Below* and Lauryn Hill's *The Miseducation of Lauryn Hill*—leaned aggressively into sounds that could be considered more palatable for a mainstream audience. Particularly in the era of their releases, when mainstream rap was seen as especially drowned in an obsession with either excessive materialism or a very specific hustler narrative, peppered with violence, the two releases allowed the stuffier academy to honor how "unique" and "unlike rap" the two albums were. Hill, with her conscious album, half-sung, kind of acoustic. And the always-inventive Outkast, pulling from old soul and funk tropes to reel in casual listeners. The two albums are phenomenal and certainly deserved their awards. Hill's was a surprise, not just because it was the first, but also because in winning, Hill had to beat out Madonna, Sheryl Crow, and

Shania Twain, artists who were beloved by the Academy and who had a history with the awards. In the year Outkast won, Missy Elliott was a nominee for her album *Under Construction*, which made the second year in a row that two rap albums were up for the award, as 2003 had both Nelly's *Nellyville* and Eminem's *The Eminem Show*. After 2004, two rap albums were not nominated for Album of the Year until a decade later, when Kendrick Lamar's *Good Kid, M.A.A.D City* was nominated next to Macklemore and Ryan Lewis's *The Heist*. Daft Punk won the award for their album *Random Access Memories*.

No rapper has ever won the award for Record of the Year or Song of the Year, and I say this knowing the politics behind awards shows, flimsy as they may be. And I say this knowing that a Grammy Award means nothing to a hood where Kendrick Lamar's music plays at a protest and urges young black organizers to push against a boundary once more. And I know a Grammy Award means nothing to that shit we rap to ourselves in our cars with our homies, or the shit we play on a basketball court during an endless summer, or the shit we use to drown out our grief or turn up our joy. To say the Grammys don't care about *the culture* is easy, but it's much more difficult to define the vastness of what that culture is and the many ways it manifests itself and brings itself to life in ways that live beyond an award. It's even harder to make peace with that, though, when the system of awards remains the only way that art is validated by an establishment.

Despite the Grammy's flimsy political standing and its strained relationship with rap, at the inception of that relationship, it was rap music that gave the Grammy Awards a crash course in political urgency. In 1989, when the Grammy's introduced a category for Best Rap Performance, there was a boycott. DJ Jazzy Jeff and the Fresh Prince won for their song "Parents Just Don't Understand," winning over other nominees Salt-N-Pepa ("Push It"), J.J. Fad ("Supersonic"), Kool Moe Dee ("Wild Wild West"), and LL Cool J ("Going Back To Cali").

When the Grammys announced that the award would be presented in a preshow segment and not televised, this caused a rift with the nominated acts and the genre at large. The Grammys supposedly recognizing that rap was more than just a category addition. It was a statement for the still-young genre, an acknowledgment that it should be taken seriously and that it had a future beyond just a handful of bright years. The establishment was sending a message that the genre should be honored as more than just an upstart. To then say that the award wouldn't be televised felt like a half measure, like putting a tray of food outside for someone starving but not offering them any shelter from the storm. Rightfully, all of the artists nominated chose to boycott the awards—except for Kool Moe Dee, who was already slated as one of the presenters. During his presentation for Best Male R&B Vocalist, he kicked a brief rhyme in the name of his boycotting peers, also attempting to paint rap in a positive light. Because, make no mistake, that is also what this was about, and perhaps what it has been about since: the Grammys' Recording Academy attempting to sell rap through the lens of respectability. Moe Dee's presence was an antiboycott in some ways. Then an elder statesman of the genre, he felt it was his responsibility to put rap music on the map the best he could in his allotted time. So he took to the mic, even briefly setting aside his then-still-brewing feud with LL Cool J, though not mentioning him by name:

> *On the behalf of all MCs,*
> *my co-workers and fellow nominees*
>
> *Jazzy Jeff, J.J. Fad,*
> *Salt-N-Pepa and the boy who's bad*
>
> *We personify power and a drug-free mind,*
> *and we express ourselves through rhythm and rhyme*
>
> *So I think it's time that the whole world knows*
> *rap is here to stay. Drummer, let's go.*

Meanwhile, in another corner of Los Angeles, then–Def Jam–heads Russell Simmons and Lyor Cohen held a party, boycotting the Grammys. *Yo! MTV Raps* was there. All of the other nominees attended, as well as other artists seen as hip-hop royalty. The Grammys were charged with treating hip-hop like a stepchild and "ghettoizing" the genre, according to Def Jam spokesperson Bill Adler. In an era before social media, the boycott still made waves, becoming one of the biggest stories of Grammy night. The Grammys were dismissive at the moment, making a statement about the number of categories versus the time allotted to air them. ("When you have 76 Grammy categories and only time to put 12 on air, you're going to have 64 unhappy groups of people," a Grammy spokesperson said the night before the show aired.)

But rap won its small battle, simply by denying access. The Grammys knew that if they were to acknowledge rap music going forward, they would actually need the artists on board. It was a loud statement made by the rappers who didn't attend—one that said, if you want the access to our culture, you actually have to honor it and honor it loudly, because we're not going anywhere. Because rap was such a young genre at the time, and all of the rappers participating in the boycott were so young, the stakes were high. Even though it seemed that there was confidence in the outcome of the boycott, it seemed just as likely that the Grammy Awards might have decided that rap music wasn't worth the trouble and dismissed it wholeheartedly in years going forward.

They didn't of course. Rap categories were expanded in the following years, including Best Rap Song and Best Rap Album, with at least one of the categories being televised each year until 2015, when rap was inexplicably left out of the televised broadcast.

In some ways, rap's relationship with the Grammys has always been tainted by its original protest of them. The Grammy Awards treat rap like it should be lucky to be there, because in the eyes of the establishment, it seems to always imagine that it is doing rap a favor. Rap was ungrateful early, so the Grammy Awards threw rap a bone, and in exchange, rap music has to be the deeply thankful subordinate, bowing at the throwing of the award and asking for scraps, even as the often-white music world around rap music gets rewarded for borrowing from its sounds, aesthetics, and tropes. When a rapper is nominated for one of the major awards now, most in the community of rap fans don't expect a win, and yet our hearts still break when watching the sadness of someone like Kanye West, who went 0 for 3 on Album of the Year wins after being nominated three times in a row for his brilliant run of three albums, *The College Dropout*, *Late Registration*, and *Graduation*. The loss is expected but still mourned. This is a genre that caters directly to a people who have spent their lives mourning the loss they always knew was coming.

When the 1989 Grammy boycott took place, A Tribe Called Quest hadn't released an album yet. They weren't at the boycott, but it's safe to imagine that they might have been, had it taken place a year, or two years, or five years later. A Tribe Called Quest didn't get nominated for a Grammy Award during the run when they made their most critically successful albums: *People's Instinctive Travels*, *The Low End Theory*, and *Midnight Marauders* all flew under the Grammy Awards radar. They weren't nominated for a Grammy Award until 1997, when *Beats, Rhymes and Life* found itself nominated for Best Rap Album, and the album's lead single, "1nce Again," was nominated for Best Rap Performance by a Duo or Group. The album lost to *The Score* by Fugees, and the song lost to "Crossroads" by Bone Thugs. In 1999, Tribe was nominated one more time. *The Love Movement* was nominated for Best Rap Album, losing to Jay-Z's *Vol. 2 . . . Hard Knock Life*. In all years of their nominations, Tribe chose to sit out the Grammy Awards, not attending as guests.

In February of 2017, Tribe was on stage at the Grammy

Awards for the first time. The awards that night had already proven to be overwhelmed with tension and awkward moments. It was now three months after Donald Trump's election, and almost one month since his inauguration. The Americans who first walked around in a haze of shock and misery were just now beginning to snap out of it and come to terms with the world around them being the world they were in. It must be said that for several marginalized communities, this world was all too familiar—something many of us had been living under for years, even before Trump took office. Still, there were newer fears to navigate, and newer ways to resist, and new people along for the ride, needing to be both shepherded and watched anxiously. We were all just settling into the new normal: news alerts flying at us from every direction, and almost always with bad news. Now, less than a year later, we're used to it. We wake up, sigh, scroll through the news and imagine the various ways that our undoing might arrive. But in February 2017, the exhaustion was new.

The Grammys came at a very particular time, as well: The Dakota Access Pipeline protests came to a head in February. The protests, which began in April 2016, were finally being broken apart by police and the military, even after some moments of hope throughout. The fight ignited around the building of the Dakota Access Pipeline in the spring of 2016. The pipeline is 1,172 miles long, cutting through land in both North and South Dakota before ending up in Patoka, Illinois. The oil pipeline route, at the time of its proposal, was set to cut across land of spiritual and cultural significance for the Lakota Nation and other surrounding nations in the Dakotas.

The pipeline was opposed not just for the impact it would have on cultural and spiritual spaces but also for the very obvious environmental risks: oil spills contaminating the water that people in these communities used to fulfill their everyday needs. The Standing Rock Sioux tribe was the most visible in the protests, and young members of the tribe were on the front lines of the protests, remaining the face of the #NoDAPL campaign that captured the attention of social media and drew the world's eyes to the small revolution. The protest was long and arduous, with many people camping out on the land and refusing to move in the face of police violence and military threats. In September 2016, construction workers bulldozed land that the tribe had identified as sacred ground. When protesters pushed into the area to protect it, attack dogs were unleashed on them, biting some of the protesters. The incident was recorded and placed on YouTube, where it went viral. In October, police with riot gear and military soldiers used excessive force to clear an encampment in the pipeline's path. It was a violent clearing, and was again recorded for the world to see.

It is one thing to throw your hands in the air and say "the world is burning again, oh the world is burning," but to see a people fight for access to clean water in the face of a very particular American greed is haunting. By November, people from all over the country joined the protests, making the trek from wherever they were to North Dakota. By December, crowds of protesters from all over were fighting off the brutal cold occupying the land every day, unmoving.

But by January 24, 2017, mere days after his inauguration, Donald Trump signed an executive order to advance the construction of the pipeline. By February 7, Trump advised the army engineers to proceed with the pipeline at all costs. Less than a week later, protesters were being forcefully removed from the land. All of them would be gone by the end of the month. There was briefly power to the people, and then not. At a time when people needed to believe that they had the capacity within themselves to change things, all that was left was the hollow echo of empire, molding the land, again, into whatever it wants.

If there was a year for the Grammy Awards to be staunchly and explicitly political, it was 2017. If there was a year to write a large check and attempt to cash it on stage, it was this one, when so many people felt like the ability to entertain was a luxury, when I needed to see someone, anyone, taking a risk while the stakes were high for them, or even higher for someone they may care about. What we got, for much of the show, was a performative bore.

When Katy Perry stands in front of the US Constitution projected on a screen and tells us that we need unity, I'm left to ask about the "we"—and if I am in the universal "we," with whom am I being asked to unify? Paris Jackson takes to the stage and awkwardly pronounces the "NoDAPL" hashtag as though she'd just heard it for the first time moments before taking to the stage. There were vague pronouncements about "everything that's been going on" and "the world we're in," but no one named names. No one made themselves large enough to seem impenetrable.

And then there was A Tribe Called Quest.

As legends in their final act with a dead member, A Tribe

Called Quest could have arrived at the Grammy Awards and played the old hits, even with a sterling new album in their back pocket. That's the thing. No one *needed* A Tribe Called Quest to be the ones to finally wrestle a real political moment out of the Grammy Awards, but there they were. Times were urgent—a moment for people to say what they really meant and leave nothing to chance. Leave it to rap, once neglected by the Grammys and then tediously embraced, to flip that switch. Every piece of A Tribe Called Quest's Grammy performance was calculated, sharp, and, most importantly, openly angry—led by an artist, Q-Tip, who was clearly uninterested in wasting time. Introducing their performance, Q-Tip spoke the group into existence as a single body speaking for "all those people around the world, all those people who are pushing people in power to represent them." It is a bold statement, and its spirit—devoid of self-service—runs counter to the general mood of the Grammys. But Q-Tip's newfound urgency makes him believable as someone willing to fight the fight next to you, even if only from a stage miles away.

Halfway through Tribe's performance, the voice and presence of Busta Rhymes arrived, taking direct aim at Donald Trump, whom he called "President Agent Orange," and stating that he was "not feeling the current political climate." The performance of the song was perfect. The chorus echoes and parodies his campaign promises; it is an unblinking anthem that strips the mask off of intolerance and fear and reveals the naked face, plain and ugly.

The song's finest moment is a verse by Phife Dawg, which, that night, echoed throughout the arena while A Tribe Called

Quest stood onstage with Busta, Consequence, and Anderson Paak, all of them with fists raised. When the song finally died down, there was Q-Tip at the center of the stage in all black, only briefly lit up by the thin gold chain around his neck, shouting the same word over and over: *Resist. Resist. Resist.*

It is a silly thing we do, attach awards to art and then judge it by what it can or can't win. It runs counter to why so many of us first mine our passions for music. It is, perhaps, even more silly that a show like the Grammy Awards can suck us in with this model, promising a spectacle that feeds into the industry-wide reliance on crown-giving and gatekeeping. But if we must keep doing this, in these times particularly, thank God for A Tribe Called Quest. Everyone does not need to approach home plate, but for those who do, the time for watching pitches sail by is long over. Q-Tip watched time run out on his beloved friend and bandmate, and, I imagine, he could see the end for A Tribe Called Quest. What this has awakened in him is the ability to take big swings without fear. Tribe's performance was the first rap performance on the Grammy stage in the era of this new presidency. It added to a lineage of statement performances by rappers at the Grammy Awards in recent years, but it was direct, jarring. When it was over, it did feel like it was for the people. It did feel like a group, for a moment, tearing the target from the backs of the endangered masses and putting it on its own chest.

Months later, in November of 2017, Q-Tip is on an Instagram video, frantically pacing in his kitchen while jazz fusion plays in the background. The Grammy Award nominations had been announced that morning, and to the surprise of many, A Tribe Called Quest was not nominated for a single award. The fact that they would be nominated seemed like a foregone conclusion after their stunning performance, but it also seemed that even if they weren't, Q-Tip maybe wouldn't care much.

In a long, several-video rant that was later deleted, Q-Tip begins by saying "Bismillah A Rahman A Rahim," meaning "In the name of Allah, the most beneficent, the most merciful." It is a gentle blessing for the wave of emotion that followed: Tip lamenting the Grammy Awards structure and goals, defending his album in the wake of applause surrounding the Grammys for being more diverse.

"Y'all think it's a caveat because a white man wasn't nominated in no major categories and shit? We were the most black, cultured group out. That's all we stood on. That's what we represented. This last Tribe album, this stands with everyone else's shit that's up there. I don't give a fuck."

He took aim at the history of the awards, pointing out all the legendary artists who had never received one: Jimi Hendrix, Led Zeppelin, Marvin Gaye.

But what was most telling in the reaction was the moment when Tip, exhausted, recalled the Grammy performance from months earlier.

"Y'all fuckin' busted y'all ass to try and get us out there and perform! You think a nigga wanted to fuckin' go out there and perform after I lost my man? We closed y'all show and we don't get no fucking nominations? The last Tribe album? My man is gone!"

The other parts are perhaps more sensational and historically on point, but for anyone who has ever had to mourn, this is the part that stood out. The way Tip's voice broke from anger to sadness when briefly reinviting Phife into the room. The way he fought through the statement, as he had fought through the past several months since the album's release without his friend by his side. This isn't how it was supposed to be. He wasn't supposed to have gone on a tour without Phife, and he wasn't supposed to perform at the Grammy Awards without Phife by his side, and he definitely wasn't supposed to be fighting for the validity of his album without his brother Malik there to push him forward.

It isn't as if Q-Tip had hidden his pain before that moment, it was just that he had never peeled back the layers intensely until them. It was brief—he gathered himself and continued his rage at the Grammys shortly after. But it was a moment when one was reminded of the void, and how that void shifted the stakes of the album. And in the moment, it seemed foolish to imagine that Q-Tip wouldn't have cared if they didn't get nominated. Of course he cared, more than anything. It wasn't just for his legacy anymore. It never was.

I spent a lot of 2017 in schools, and I imagine that I will spend a lot of future years in schools. Because of this, I spend a lot of time talking to people younger than I am, and I spend a lot of time talking to them about music. This creates an interesting discussion point for me—I spent 2017 finding myself remembering that when I was young and wanted to talk to someone older about music, I mostly wanted validation that the thing I liked was not, in fact, awful. This had mixed results in my teenage years. My love of the so-called "shiny suit era" had its detractors, many of them older than me, many of them longing for the days of what they imagined to be "real hip-hop."

The question I spent most of my time answering in 2017 was how I felt about what is now called "mumble rap" in the popular discourse—rappers who eschew lyrical prowess in the name of drum-heavy trap beats and melodic choruses. If there is one thing that is for sure, changing trends in music will forever have their scapegoats, and because the trends in rap music shift so rapidly, scapegoats appear and then are replaced by new scapegoats nearly every two or three years. Shiny suit rap was a scapegoat once, back after Biggie was murdered and Tupac was murdered before that, and conservative media outlets were delighting in what surely was soon to be the death of the genre they hated most. But then songs about money and partying and living like no death would ever arrive for you ended up on the radio. Auto-Tune was a scapegoat for a while, until Kanye West made *808s and Heartbreak* in 2008, and people decided Auto-Tune was a worthwhile artistic endeavor until Jay-Z released the song "Death of Auto-Tune" in the summer of 2009, and then it was done for good.

"Mumble rap" is the most active and vigorous scapegoat rap has had in years, in part because the internet—particularly social media—has created a landscape for it to thrive and be a hotly debated topic, engaging in the ideas of language and whether or not rappers should have to adhere to them, or whether or not this so-called mumble rap is actually pushing the genre forward, past some of its bowing to establishments.

The real truth is that the rappers don't actually mumble. Rappers like Lil Yachty, Lil Uzi Vert, and Young Thug aren't really aesthetically or sonically similar, and all of them rap fairly clearly. What people are really angling at is the drug-drenched persona of young rappers who seem to have no substance, as they put it. What people are really pointing at is what they believe to be a lack of lyricism. I don't necessarily rebuke this in its entirety, but I rebuke the idea that my pals and I weren't young once and didn't listen to shit that moved us to dance or get reckless no matter what the rapper was saying. I rebuke the idea that every lyric written when I was a young hip-hop lover was sent down from the heavens and written with a golden pen. I rebuke the idea that the "turn up" is new or something that anyone in need of it should be ashamed of. Or the idea that the turn up isn't flexible. That it doesn't happen in the middle of a gospel song on Sunday, or in a trap house on any day when people in the hood get paid, or in a nightclub in New York when the horn player catches a good solo and the band lets him air it out until he's gotten all he can out of his instrument.

And so, young people want to ask me what I think about mumble rap. Some of them wait eagerly, hoping I'll validate their interests. Some—the ones I find more interesting—bemoan the state of hip-hop now, and wonder if it's crumbling due to this new faction of young rappers largely existing in a haze of drugs and excess.

I am trying not to be the elder that I had access to in my days of young rap fandom. For them, it was the 1980s that was the holy grail, and everything in the late 1990s was a horn signaling the death of a genre. I don't think that is where we are now. Some of the young people I talk to aren't sure what so-called "real hip-hop" is, but they know enough to know what it isn't. Early in the year, many of them had never heard of A Tribe Called Quest, and then later, only knew them as a phoenix, risen from the ashes—though they were unsure what the ashes were or how they got there. So many people have an idea of what "real hip-hop" is, or the standards of what it should adhere to, and that makes the genre narrow. So narrow, in fact, that many of those people can't see the disciples of Tribe right in front of them. Artists like Anderson Paak, who joined Tribe on stage during their Grammy performance in 2017, eagerly drumming along with his heroes. Or even someone like Joey Bada$$, or Isaiah Rashad, or Danny Brown. Lineage is most important to preserve in rap music. It isn't always what you hear on the surface, but what you hear trying to claw its way out. Tribe made it easy for all of us with jazz, but it's not like that anymore. You really gotta want to sit down with an album. And I know, I know it's hard to do, with one album leaving just in time for another to arrive. But if there is something that I know about whatever I imagine real hip-hop to be, it's that it demands patience from a listener. It demands someone willing to sit awhile and let the music enter them.

I don't tell young rap fans that, though. I tell them that I'm trying to get into the songs they're into, and I am. I tell them that I listen to stuff that people younger than me are listening to because I never want to be out of line and out of touch.

I want to know where rap is going, and I want to always be able to accept it, or at least find a path to acceptance, no matter how long or winding it is. I tell them that I like Lil Uzi Vert, and I do. I think that in ten years' time, though, none of this will matter. Genre is going to be a thing of the past soon anyway, man. It's all gonna be pop music before too long, so you might as well enjoy your safe houses now while you've got 'em. I tell the rap fans younger than me who don't know it yet that A Tribe Called Quest made rap music that they might think is real enough. That it was just beats and rhymes—no gimmicks. That's still happening now, too. The dream isn't over yet. Find something you love before everything is washed away by a wave of sound pushing all rap closer and closer to the dreaded radio. Everything reaching for the pop charts. I tell young rap fans who haven't heard it to listen to *Midnight Marauders*, to the way "Steve Biko" falls effortlessly into "Award Tour" and the small burst of marching and playful horns that feel like an endless summer coming. I tell young rap fans that they might have liked Phife, the eternal underdog—small, and yet still somehow towering. I tell them that at least we still have Q-Tip, who—even after all this time—is committed solely to his massive and impossible visions.

And we may never have anyone as great as them again. The idea of the rap group isn't entirely gone, and it might go through another cycle—especially now, with the rise of groups like Migos and Rae Sremmurd. But a group like A Tribe Called Quest will never exist again. And what a tragic but perfect ending to what they gave. Of course there had to be a funeral. Of course there had to be a death during a dark year, painting the months even darker, and of course there had to be an album pushed into a country that needed it right as it arrived, and of course there had to be a performance on music's largest stage with black fists raised in the air. Not every story in music ends with a group forced to throw in the towel due to a great and impossible loss, and not every story should. But had it not, I would want A Tribe Called Quest to return again and again, giving me the doses of updated nostalgia that I might need when no other music could provide it. At least now, I think, we can lay them to rest.

The music video for "The Space Program" came out right as the summer of 2018 got especially hot along the coasts. Right as New Yorkers said fuck it and crowded indoors by their fans and window A/C units. That "too hot to touch another person, no matter what the body desires" weather. It was the final Tribe video, released well over a year after their final album. It is a frantic and hectic visual, with Q-Tip, Ali, and Jarobi fighting to break free from a spaceship while also traversing a vast desert. Phife's verse in the song is mouthed by a line of brilliant cameos from the group's longtime peers: Erykah Badu, Questlove, Pharrell. At the end of the video, the viewer sees the group walking through the desert and into the sunset, before the three bodies become a blur. One might be reminded of the closing scene in the group's first video, "I Left My Wallet in El Segundo," which ended with the group, then a foursome, walking into the desert heat and becoming small. Once, they were young and aching to go home. Now, they are old, and simply looking to vanish into anywhere but here. A blur, swallowed by a horizon.

We can go about speaking the name of A Tribe Called Quest as we might speak the name of someone from our distant past who changed our way of seeing. If I close my eyes now, I think I see the world as A Tribe Called Quest would have had me see it. I think I can see my people dancing in the streets, like nothing they loved has ever been set on fire.

There are not enough roses in the world for me to lay at the feet of this impossible group, but I hope this effort counts. I hope Phife can see all of us still trying, from wherever he may be. I hope Q-Tip knows that he's done something great. I hope when the time comes for the generation after mine to talk about what's real, they'll pull a Tribe CD out of their pockets, worn down from a decade's use and perhaps an older sibling. I hope they'll put it in a CD player and let a room be carried away.

Acknowledgments

Thanks to Casey Kittrell for hanging out with me in Austin one spring afternoon in 2017 and pushing me to give this book a shot. Thanks to all of the staff and editors at the University of Texas Press for working with me on this project and helping it come out as stellar as possible. Thanks, as always, to Jessica Hopper, my once and forever boss. To Cheryl-Boyce Taylor for her generosity, her poems, her wisdom, and her kindness. To A Tribe Called Quest for allowing a landscape for me to make sense of the troubled times in my past, in my present, and undoubtedly in my future. This book is for Malik.